Y0-DDO-846

I'M STUCK

AND I CAN'T GET OUT

Learning What It
Takes To Move Forward

KEVIN R. BAIRD, D.MIN.

AMOS 9 - 13 - 15

11/6/23

Copyright © 2019 by Kevin R. Baird, D.Min.

All rights reserved. This book is protected by the copyright laws of the United States of America. This book may not be copied or reprinted for commercial gain or profit. The use of short quotations or occasional page copying for personal or group study is permitted and encouraged. Permission will be granted upon request.

Scripture quotations, unless otherwise indicatedare taken from the *Holy Bible, New King James Version,* NKJV. Copyright © 1982 by Thomas Nelson, Inc. Used by permission. All rights reserved.

FIRST EDITION

ISBN: 978-1-946466-73-0

Library of Congress: 2019913257

Published by

Certa PUBLISHING

3741 Linden Avenue SE | Grand Rapids, MI 49548

Printed in the United States of America

Disclaimer: The views and opinions expressed in this book are solely those of the author and other contributors. These views and opinions do not necessarily represent those of Certa Publishing. Please note that Certa Publishing's publishing style capitalizes certain pronouns in Scripture that refer to the Father, Son, and Holy Spirit, and may differ from some publishers' styles.

Endorsements

First and foremost, Dr. Kevin Baird is a man of excellent spirit and profound wisdom. Out of his understanding and wisdom, he accurately describes what it means to be "stuck" in a hard place where all victory seems to be lost and all hope is gone! He gives great examples of being stuck in ruts of disappointments and setbacks where there seems to be no ability to move forward. Dr. Baird is a messenger of hope as he gives simple steps in coming out of the ruts of our hard places—moving forward, no looking back, being a risk taker, and knowing that a better day is coming because our loving Father always has the last word!

Dr. Rod Aguillard
Senior Overseer, Network of Related Pastors
Reserve, Louisiana

When confusing and difficult circumstances shake us to the core, it's only natural to feel afraid and stuck. But what if we could learn to find God's goodness and providence in the midst of the desperateness of our circumstances? I'm so thankful for my father, Kevin, and the wisdom and transparency he pours out in this book. I love the calm reassurances and biblical truth he shares as he unpacks his own journey of pastoring and leading people. I've had a front row seat for years, watching dad model faithfulness, godliness, and obedience through every season. It's, in turn, made me a better man. If you feel *stuck* and desire to move forward, then go ahead and begin reading… because this book is for you.

Rev. Clayton Baird
Teaching Pastor, Celebration Church
Co-Host, The BAIRD & BAIRD Podcast
Jacksonville, Florida

It's with great delight that I recommend Dr. Kevin Baird's newest book, *I'm Stuck And I Can't Get Out.* As someone blessed to invest in leaders worldwide, I have a two-fold observation. First, books containing the latest leadership theories and "hip" revelation of the day are plentiful; but there are FEW books written by leaders who actually bear the scars, maintained their integrity, and actually have something transformative to say. Second, as a sign of the times it seems that many leaders are discouraged and holding on to their calling by a thread. Books like this one are life-changing and can breathe fresh faith and vision back into your soul! In *I'm Stuck And I Can't Get Out*, Dr. Baird leverages real life examples. He not only defines what it means to be *stuck*, but he invites us to broaden our perspective by asking critical questions and then lays out a clear and life-giving path forward toward our life's purpose and journey of faith. Simply put *I'm Stuck And I Can't Get Out* is practical, achievable, and powerful! Join me in getting this book into the hands of today's leaders… we need it!!

Dr. Randal S. Langley,
CEO, Christian Life Global Leaders Network
President, Christian Life School of Theology/Global
Pensacola, Florida

Dr. Kevin Baird is a solid Christian man, minister, and theologian. That is quite apparent as you read this amazing book. He doesn't just teach from his incredible knowledge of the Word, but from much fire-tested experience. If you are going through trials, this book will inspire you to hold on. If you are currently not going through one, this book will equip you with sound biblical principles to prepare for whatever the enemy throws at you. God is using my friend, Kevin, to help people get out of what they're stuck in!

Rev. Terry Wong
Senior Pastor, Calvary Assembly of God
Presbyter, Hawaii Assemblies of God
Honolulu, Hawaii

Questions. Questions. Questions. Sadly, we keep these questions to ourselves. It is very healing to have a voice that brings forward ways and understanding of how to get "unstuck." I commend this work to every reader not as a theoretical, but as a reality to me. Pastor Baird's ministry helped me transition through a very difficult period recently with the essence of the concepts in this work. Read. Soak. Apply. You won't regret it.

Alan Bragwell, M.A., N.C.C., L.P.C.-S.
Director, Bragwell Services
Florence, Alabama

One of the most challenging places a person can find themselves in is what I call the "no-man's land," where one does not know where to go or what to do. In those moments, life is quite puzzling and discouraging. Often the future path is unclear and troubling. Kevin Baird has produced what I consider the best description, analysis, and practical guideline for people who find themselves stuck in the puzzling conundrums of life. Frankly, all humans have experienced some aspect of these perplexing moments. The reader will find that Kevin has amazingly articulated the thoughts, emotions, and questions that arise in all of us during those occasions. One of the best features of this book is the well-balanced approach between biblical examples, contemporary illustrations, and practical advice. The reader will certainly find this book to be one of the best works on the subject and one worth reading several times.

Dr. Charles H. Gaulden
Professor of Religion, Southeastern University
Lakeland, Florida

I'm Stuck And I Can't Get Out deep dives beyond mere platitudes into the heart of the matter concerning real world issues all people face in their quest for significance in life. If you enjoy mediocrity and defeatism, this book is not for you; however, if your desire is to find a place of true fulfillment, escape the sand bars, and find the open seas, enjoy the journey as Dr. Baird helps you navigate past the frustrations of the soul into the depths of the spirit. This work speaks to anyone at any station of life and will benefit every Christian believer from the newly born to the seasoned saint. It will have you "stuck" to its pages as you find yourself laughing, wiping a tear, and relating to this surprisingly ascendant path to purpose. Dr. Baird teaches you how to turn your crucible of frustration into a veritable cruise liner, moving you past "stuck" to sailing again. So enjoy this journey as you realize that earthly trials are mere light afflictions compared to the glory that awaits you, just beyond your next horizon.

Dr. Doug Bankson
Senior Pastor, Victory Church World Outreach Center
Vice Mayor, Apopka, Florida

None of us are exempt from seasons in life where we seem to be paralyzed. In spite of our previous victories and accomplishments, the enemy, at times, declares 'checkmate' over our present and future. It leaves us without strength or direction to move forward. In this book, Dr. Kevin Baird draws from his years of experience in life and ministry to deliver a powerful premise. It is during these "stuck" times that we are being tested to the degree of our value to the Kingdom. May every reader hear the Spirit say, "It is time to arise, move forward, and succeed."

Dr. Carl Morris
Senior Pastor, Abundant Life Church
Florence, South Carolina

Dr. Kevin Baird is a true man of God that I have come to love and respect very deeply over the last many years. He has stood on the mountaintop. He has trekked through the valleys. He understands life with the struggles, the triumphs, and how to apply instructions that were left to us by our Creator in the Holy Scriptures. I highly recommend that you carefully, thoughtfully, and prayerfully consider the wisdom contained in this writing.

Rev. Cary Gordon
Senior Pastor, Cornerstone World Outreach
Author, Radio Host, Film Producer
Sioux City, Iowa

Acknowledgments

After writing my first book, I have come to the conclusion that getting it into print and publication is most closely analogous to selling your house. Many people initially think that they can broker a house sale on their own. However, they soon realize into the process that thought is not only a foolish one, but indeed there are numerous and nameless people invested in its successful closing. *I'm Stuck And I Can't Get Out* may have been my idea, but without those numerous and nameless people, these pages would not be in your hands.

At the top of the recognition list has to be my wife and life partner, Tracie. She has, for over thirty-seven years, walked every inch of most of the stories found in this book. She has exhorted, encouraged, suggested, prayed, and prophesied over this project. She epitomizes a woman of God of the highest order and I am blessed to call her mine.

A special thanks goes to my publishers Pat and Sheila McGuffin, who coached me and encouraged me through to completion. Without Pat's willingness to mentor me in this writing endeavor, this book would simply be another file on my laptop.

I am grateful for the former members of Legacy Church, Charleston, South Carolina, who consistently urged me to get this book written for over twenty years. It took longer than it should have, but your affirmation has finally found expression in these pages.

And to my Savior and King, Jesus Christ, who solicits my highest allegiance and love—the best decision I ever made was over forty years ago when I said "yes" and responded to His amazing grace and experienced His transformational power. The journey has been a crazy adventure, but I would do it all again if I could.

To God our Savior, Who alone is wise, be glory and majesty, dominion and power, both now and forever. Amen. (Jude 1:25)

Table Of Contents

Introduction

"I just can't see a way forward from this situation."
"Is this my fault, God's fault, or the devil's fault?"

"Did the Lord lead me to this place?"

"If God is sovereign and can do anything, why doesn't He do something about my circumstances now?"

"Is He waiting on me to do something or am I to wait on Him?"

"How did I even get here?"

"How do I get out?"

"Did I miss some instruction, some warning sign, or some guidance?"

"Where are You, God?"

"How do I even begin to untangle this moment?"

"Are there any steps to move forward from this place?"

"Will I be stuck in this circumstance forever?"

A pastor is supposed to have all the answers to all the mysteries of life. At least that is the assumption many people carry, including most clergy. As with nearly all pastors, I have been trained and mentored and have certain experiences that supposedly qualify me to input a wide variety of situations. In most circumstances, those foundations give me a pretty good basis to offer wisdom and counsel to people. However, there are moments in every person's life, including my life, that press the person to the very edges of their understanding, wisdom, and insight—situations that are not easily answered or understood by pasting one Scripture verse on it or listening to an inspirational Christian worship song.

These moments are confusing, gut-wrenching, and candidly, frustrating. Instead of our having an answer, these moments create untold questions like the ones above. And the hardest part is the realization that people are watching you live this situation and you don't have a tidy explanation for why it is happening. After decades of vocational ministry, I came to one of those defining moments.

The church I was pastoring had been birthed through no small adversity. My wife and I were the founders and leaders of this church plant, ironically started out of a painful separation from another church in our region. We didn't plan this kind of beginning. In fact, our confident declaration for years had been that we were simply not church planters and that starting a church simply could not be the will of God under any circumstance. I suppose it might be analogous to the person who is willing to lead a corporation but would never consider being an entrepreneur and starting their own business.

The thought of starting a church from "ground zero" with nothing but a dream or a vision was simply beyond my scope of faith at the time. I remember saying on more than one occasion that I would "never" be a church planter. Nevertheless, here we were, separated from a well-established, growing work and listening to the heartfelt cries of literally scores of people asking us to stay and be their pastors. I was reminded at that moment how dangerous it is to say "never" to God. And so, with no money to begin the work, no paycheck on the horizon, and no idea of how to start a church, we launched into the greatest learning curve and faith walk of our lives up to that point. And gratefully we saw our God do untold miracles.

The coincidences (actually providences) that took place were amazing. The finances that were released at just the right moment were astounding. The open doors to ministry and worship locations were incredible. We were able to quickly hire staff to assist us in the work. And after five years, it all consummated in the miraculous purchase of more than eleven acres of prime real estate in a growing region of the city. This is the way, everyone assumed, things were supposed to go when people are serving God and doing His work. Little did we all realize, especially me, that a curveball was approaching for which I was not completely prepared. The only way I can describe this moment is by using the word *stuck*. As you will read in the ensuing chapters, suddenly what seemed to be moving along seamlessly came to a grinding halt. I was suddenly cornered in what felt to be a dead-end street with no exit, and I didn't know why and couldn't find a way out.

As in most paralyzing circumstances, there are perhaps a thousand details and emotions of this "stuck" moment, but it came to a head one evening as my wife and I were having dinner at one of our favorite pizza restaurants. She excused herself briefly to go to the ladies' room, leaving me alone to ponder my life and the ministry. As was mentioned, the church had been able to secure some prime property with indisputable divine favor. However, after such a remarkable purchase, things seemed to take an immediate turn.

The county where the church was located was known for its animosity and hostility with church building and construction—I suspect due to a loss of tax revenue. I had to deal with officials who were consistently dragging their feet in permit approvals and drawing designs. They forced me to mitigate a single oak tree on eleven acres of property for nearly a year as they pondered whether they would allow us to cut it down or not. I had to find a way to reduce another wetland mitigation fee of tens of thousands of dollars the federal government was attempting to charge us, which would ostensibly shut down any attempt at construction.

During this time a large housing bubble burst in the nation, leaving us with little equity in the property to build at our permanent location. I reached out to banks and bond companies to find an acceptable path to financing only to receive rejection replies as fear rippled through the financial sector. After untold of months of battle, I finally found a bank that would facilitate our construction loan under the stipulation that we raise an easily attained amount to demonstrate our willingness as a congregation to embrace the project.

I was confident, after watching our initial five years of miracles, that this financial number and more would be reached, only to find out that we could barely raise half of what was needed. The bank understandably rescinded its offer. It was after this that people began leaving the church, sensing their "season" was over. We were stuck, and people could sense it. I knew it too, but I didn't have an answer. I tried to look faith-filled and calm as all these dynamics started to roll out of my control. Life was beginning to feel like the proverbial snowball rolling down a mountain getting larger and more desperate as the days moved forward, but I was immobilized.

By the time my wife returned to the table at the restaurant, tears were flowing down my cheeks. The pressure and confusion of being stuck had finally begun to manifest on my face. The questions that had been coalescing in my mind for months, which I had ignored as doubt, were beginning to come to the forefront and finding their way out of my mouth. Have you ever been in such a moment— where the pressure of your circumstances have reached such a point that you prayed for escape? The only way it can be described is that you are stuck, and it feels like a death sentence.

> ❖ ❖ ❖
>
> It has been said that the caliber of a person can be determined by the amount of opposition it takes to discourage them.

It has been said that the caliber of a person can be determined by the amount of opposition it takes to discourage them. At that moment I felt as if I had reached the edge of my tolerance. My sense is that if you have read this far, then there is a high likelihood that you too have found yourself in the land of "stuck," probably asking similar questions. You may not be a pastor, but your commitment to God and the confusion and frustration of this moment are draining you on numerous levels. Perhaps you have been, like me, seated anonymously in a restaurant with tears trying to leak down your face. Perhaps you've come home from work, closed the door, and considered screaming at the ceiling in frustration. Perhaps the immoveable situation has actually produced headaches and body pains as physical symptoms of the stress you are feeling. To be stuck is a hard and relentless place. I know because I have been there more than a time or two. Life has a way of creating such places for us all.

The truth is, those whom God uses greatly and have a passion for His purposes will experience these kinds of moments. That is what this book is all about. How does a person, and perhaps most specifically a Christian, navigate those moments of being stuck in life? How do we provide answers to the questions that flood our minds at the moment of frustration and exhaustion, answers that can give us hope for the future and perhaps even help us move forward? How do we find our peace, our joy, and our hope when the situation we are in seems impossibly paralyzed?

Years ago a famous Peanuts cartoon strip featuring Charlie Brown was published dealing with one of Charlie's many moments of adversity. He remarks, "No problem is so awesome, so complicated, so fraught with danger that the average citizen can't run away from it." Charlie sums up what many people feel when it comes to dealing with tough or confusing moments in life. We human beings are hard-wired to want instant answers and deliverance from difficult circumstances. The truth is that it is not always possible.

Sometimes things are at work beyond our initial understanding and comprehension, which makes these "stuck" moments valuable. That being said, many people shut down emotionally and motivationally when they face an immobilizing moment. M. Scott Peck in his best-selling book *The Road Less Traveled* puts it well:

This is a great truth, one of the greatest truths. It is a great truth because once we truly see this truth, we transcend it. Once we truly know that life is difficult, once we truly understand and accept it, then life is no longer difficult. Because once it has been accepted, the fact that life is difficult no longer matters.

Most do not fully see this truth that life is difficult. Instead they moan more or less incessantly, noisily, or subtly, about the enormity of their problems, their burdens, and their difficulties, as if life were generally easy, as if life should be easy. They voice their belief noisily, or subtly, that THEIR difficulties represent a unique kind of affliction that should not be, and somehow has been especially visited upon them, or else upon their families, their tribe, their class, their nation, their race, or even their species, and not upon others. I know about this moaning because I have done my fair share.

Peck's point can be easily applied to those of us who have been stuck. It is universal in both its experience and pain.

We all have moaned in those moments, wondering what is happening. A businessman is stuck after opening his business to throngs of waiting customers only to find after some time that the receipts and foot traffic are down. The employee who was hired as the rising star of the company and experiences unusual favor in that ascent is now stuck at a dead-end job feeling that nobody notices what she is doing and accomplishing. The mom who feels stuck as a homemaker. The person who feels stuck as an unmarried, single young adult. The teacher who feels stuck in the classroom. The laborer who feels stuck and unable to break into management or get the promotion. The divorced person who feels stuck in the stigma of a failed marriage. The offended or wounded person who is emotionally stuck replaying and reliving injustices of the past. The infirmed person who feels stuck in their disease.

The one thing you can count on is that the place of "stuck" is an equal-opportunity location and will not discriminate based on race, gender, or economic status. Everyone eventually finds themselves stuck. How to get out and how to move forward are the million-dollar questions. Undoubtedly you, the reader, have felt that way or dare I say, *feel* that way. Even now as you are reading this introduction, in every direction you are looking you feel that you are stuck. You may be young, old, or somewhere in between, but at this moment nothing seems to be moving. It may feel that everything is collapsing. There is no momentum or movement forward. Is there anything you can do to change the situation you feel stuck in or are you consigned and appointed in some kind of maniacal plan to stay at this most difficult place?

❖ ❖ ❖

The one thing you can count on is that the place of "stuck" is an equal-opportunity location and will not discriminate based on race, gender, or economic status.

For the Christian believer these initial questions are a tad trickier than one might initially think. Why would I say that? Because if I were to tell you the end of my opening story it probably wouldn't fit into your preconceived idea of how stories like these are supposed to end in books like these. Most books written to inspire hope and motivation are filled with stories testifying to perilous situations overshadowed by impossible odds. The story ordinarily declares that at the last second of one's energy and the last thread of rope one was hanging on to, a miracle intervenes and the great turnaround takes place. There are certainly numerous stories in this book that follow that pattern because our God is indeed a miracle-working God.

But the solution to being "stuck" is not always the preconceived miracle ending to what our own personal desires may be. In fact, it might be better stated that the end of every "stuck" story has a providential ending. God is always in charge, but how He chooses to work in your circumstance may not necessarily follow the path you think it needs to take. In the case of my restaurant story, the answer was far different than what I initially thought—but no less amazing in the end. Yours will be too. God is no respecter of persons, and what He would do for me He will do for you. I encourage you to press through the book, listen to the subtle voice of the Holy Spirit, and I will get to the unusual conclusion of the pizza shop meltdown. It may be the ray of hope that leads you to your unusual conclusion.

As you will read in the following chapters, there are various kinds of "stuck" places and situations. There are various ways of navigating your way through and out of those circumstances. For me, the ability to shake loose from what felt to be inescapable was not only tied to my feelings of hope and possibility for the future, but literally how I understood my relationship with God. In other words, this is serious stuff.

I claim no special status in approaching a subject. I am as normal and as human as the next person. Disappointingly, pastors do not glow in the dark, walk on water, or have a special dispensation of grace to weather adversity any differently than the normal congregant. I can say at this point, however, that I have not only experienced my fair share of circumstances that I interpreted at that moment as being stuck, but I have pressed through and wrestled with the theology of such moments and prevailed.

How does my faith filter this challenge that is in front of me? How do I reconcile God's goodness to His people and the desperation of my circumstances? Why do I have this amazing promise yet am immobilized in this horrific circumstance? A book such as this cannot address every situation specifically that people face. The principles and illustrations, however, are certainly transferable to most situations if the reader uses his or her creative imagination and listens to the voice of the Lord as they are shared. There is a path out of your place of being stuck. This book will help map that path out for you. It may not be exactly as you currently envision it, but it is a path nonetheless. And if you choose to find it, embrace it, and walk it, you will become that disciple of a higher caliber.

PART I — I'M STUCK

Chapter One

❖❖❖

What Does It Mean To Be Stuck?

In 1964 United States Supreme Court Justice Potter Stewart was attempting to describe his threshold test for defining what the legal definition of obscenity should be. There is a natural and legal tension between constitutionally protected and unprotected speech. People, for better and worse, have differing thresholds of tolerance in such materials. How does a free society measure such things? How do you know if you have crossed the threshold into territory that is legally protected "obscenity"? Stewart's now-famous response was "I know it when I see it."

It is no stretch to suggest that a similar tension exists when it comes to defining a paralyzing life circumstance. People looking in on your situation may define it as a simple life glitch to be treated like a mere nuisance on your journey—while you, on the other hand, see it as the defining problem of your life. How do you know if you are making too big a deal out of a moment? How do you truly define a "stuck" moment? Perhaps it can be said as Justice Stewart said it—you know it when you see it.

I am a stickler for precision, however, as we begin our journey of finding a way forward from where we might find ourselves at the moment, I think it might be beneficial to define clearly this place we call "stuck." The place of being stuck is as unique and personal as the individual. It can circumstantially look a variety of different ways in a variety of people's lives depending on their unique set of circumstances. As you will see in Scripture, there is never a common circumstantial thread in the lives of God's people.

The Lord works in a variety of ways in many dramatically different situations. The Bible never formally defines the meaning of *stuck,* nor does a modern dictionary. There is no Greek word study we can do to explore the etymology of the word. In a quick Google search you will find the word linked back to its present-tense form, "stick," which is of absolutely no use except to say that I have felt as if I were getting beat by a stick, usually a large one, in some tough situations. However, "stick" as a verb in its past participle, passive form we find the concept of *stuck,* and this is important.

> ❖ ❖ ❖
> **The place of being stuck is as unique and personal as the individual.**

The passive voice is used to show interest in the person or object that *experiences* an action rather than the person or object that *performs* the action. This is critically important. In other words, the most important thing about being stuck is *you* and not necessarily what is happening to you. I like the phrase we often use to help people maintain their perspective in challenging moments. We tell them, "Everything temporal is subject to change." What is happening to you will change eventually. The more important part is what may be at work in you. Keep that closely in mind as you continue reading this book.

It was American writer and journalist Allen Saunders who in a 1957 issue of *Reader's Digest* created the famous line "Life happens." It is true—life is what takes place while we are in the midst of executing our well-laid plans. No one signs up for getting stuck. There is no seminar to achieve this virtue of getting stuck. "Stuck" is simply life happening when you least expect it and most probably are unprepared for it. It is like the time I received a letter in the mail telling me I had won one of four prizes listed in the letter and the only requirement was to listen to a "short" sales presentation. Three of the four prizes were phenomenal, and one was a set of knives. You can always count on the fact that should you attend one of those presentations, they will last twice as long as advertised and at the end you always get the knife set. You were stuck in a situation you couldn't get out of and the prize was something you didn't really want or need. That's one analogy of the concept of "stuck"—you are in a forced immobilization with no real reward.

I have developed my own definition for this book's purpose.

STUCK — "The spiritual, psychological, or emotional inability to move forward."

It is the moment that for any one of a number of reasons you simply cannot muster the external or internal resources to press forward.

After thirty-five years of pastoring I have seen "stuck" circumstances manifest it's toll in a number of ways. Some have told me that they feel that they are in a spiritually "dry time." Others have used the terms of being stuck as a "wilderness," "cave," or the "back side of the desert." Some have suggested feelings of depression or even mid-life crisis. Those who are in addictive challenges say that they are "cycling" or internally circling around and unable to break out of their destructive patterns. A "stuck" person can take on numerous forms and looks, but the bottom line is that they feel incapacitated from getting out and moving on. They are internally and externally immobilized.

> ❖ ❖ ❖
>
> Being *stuck* is that moment, for any number of reasons, you simply cannot muster the external or internal resources to press forward.

I received a note from a friend on one occasion who works as a professional mental health provider to predominantly CEO's and business owners, which perhaps sums what I am trying to communicate best when he wrote,

> I want to thank you for your recent sermon series on "Seasons." As a professional health provider, one of the biggest problems I see is the inability of people to transition seasons of life. We are living in a time where things change at an unprecedented pace. Old, dysfunctional, lumbering systems, organizations, companies are getting clobbered. What was state of the art ten years ago is now obsolete. People are reeling. Some cannot change or transition and in turn, are stuck at a place professionally and emotionally that circumvents them from their future.

One of my favorite movies that my wife and I have watched together is *You've Got Mail*. Before the men reading this book judge my manliness based on that confession, let me say that my wife and I like the movie for totally different reasons. For her it is a romantic comedy of two unlikely people finding love after initially disliking one another. For me it is replete with wonderful illustrations concerning business and relationships that have completed many a sermon.

The story revolves around a woman, Kathleen, whose mother started an independent book-selling business years ago and named the store "The Shop Around the Corner." It was a frequent gathering place for the neighborhood people and children to fellowship and purchase their favorite books. Kathleen inherited the store after her mother's death and is now running it. It is her life and love and represents all the fond memories she had growing up with her mother and living in the neighborhood. Then enters a man named Joe Fox, who is planning to open a new book mega-superstore just around the corner from Kathleen. The movie chronicles their animosity-turned-romance as Fox Books puts The Shop Around the Corner out of business.

In the middle of the movie you see how Kathleen must now wrestle with how her plans concerning The Shop Around the Corner are grinding to a halt. She had a vision for the future concerning her bookstore and it was quickly getting destroyed. She is emotionally stuck, disappointed, and cannot move forward. A dream has seemingly died. It is challenging every aspect of her being, despite the scenario of its being a common happening in business life all over America and the globe.

She fights back in every way possible but to no avail until finally the store closes. Her "stuck" circumstances appear to have won. What should have been a typical "David vs. Goliath" story with the small guy winning the day over the giant turns out exactly the opposite. The giant has won.

Now obviously, this being a romantic comedy, her victory manifests in the end as both Joe and Kathleen fall in love with one another. Her "stuck" moment of painful defeat starts to make sense, or her feelings are at least mitigated by this new relationship and presumed marriage, which will make her Mrs. Joe Fox and co-participant in the corporate bookstore. Wouldn't we all love this type of movie ending in our circumstances? And truth be told, your current moment of being stuck can have a similar outcome if you understand the dynamics of what is occurring.

It should come as no surprise that as a pastor and a committed Christian, I have derived my worldview and perspective from the Scriptures. As is the case concerning numerous subjects of which we would love to know God's thoughts, the Bible unfortunately is not written as a catalog with easily accessible chapters dealing with important information we may need. There is no table of contents that points us to the marriage book or the parenting chapter to instantly turn to in the Scriptures. There are no dating chapters or a book specifically titled "Rehabilitation." So it should come as no surprise to find out that there is no letter to those stuck in Macedonia or a book titled "First and Second Quagmire."

The Bible is a book that records in a majority of instances the stories of human beings on a journey with God. I am astounded by how many of these stories are instances of people feeling stuck and how they decided to navigate their situation. Some of them did amazingly well, while others not so much. The key to many of their successes was their ability to recognize and navigate a "stuck" moment. It might be beneficial as we begin to review just a few, for example:

Stuck In A Health Crisis:
Blind Bartimaeus (Mark 10:46–52)

Here is a man seemingly stuck in his blindness. He could not see, and his only recourse was to sit by the road begging to solicit the compassion and generosity of those who walked by. I cannot help but think of the multiple times I have pulled up to intersections with stoplights or exited an interstate highway and noticed a person with a sign begging for help. In the day we live in and the news exposés most of us have seen, we are appropriately skeptical at times in our appraisals of how needy these people may actually be. In Bartimaeus's case, however, this was not the case because he was genuinely blind and in first-century context his options were few. I define this as being stuck in a legitimate health crisis.

There is nothing that will change our plans and detour us in a different direction faster than a health issue. It is understandable at a human level to extend compassion upon those who are facing tremendous adversity in their health. And yet at the same time there is also the recognition of when we are "stuck" and our passivity is leading us to stay there. I have seen people through the years remain emotionally and spiritually seized when given a challenging diagnosis and prognosis. They let the disease or the malady determine their future.

Many people in recent years have been introduced to a man named Nick Vujicic. Nick was born without arms or legs due to an extremely rare congenital disorder known as phocomelia. Yet despite that adversity, Nick has determined not to be "stuck" in life. He is married to a wonderful woman and has two incredible children. He is a painter, swimmer, skydiver, and motivational speaker. You can easily search his story on the Internet, but let it suffice to say that he is a man much like Bartimaeus. He had a health challenge that provided adequate excuses to stay "stuck," and despite not being healed, he found the way to move forward.

Stuck In Cultural And Religious Prejudices: Nicodemus (John 3:1–21)

Nicodemus was an influential and respected member of the Jewish Sanhedrin. This group of Jewish leaders were not only well educated but also well connected and wealthy. Despite all the earthly trappings that might make a person feel empowered with numerous opportunities, he was stuck in lifeless religion and cultural tradition. He recognized this and slipped away at night to explore and learn more from this one called Jesus. It was this interaction that gave us perhaps the most famous verse in all of Scripture—John 3:16. Nicodemus illustrates those stuck in both their spiritual, cultural, and perhaps even ethnic bondages.

Of the thirty-five years I was a pastor, twenty-two were spent in Charleston, South Carolina. Charleston is a city where ethnic and religious bondages run deep and are powerful even 150 years after the great Civil War. No matter the skin pigmentation, ethnic origin, or religious tradition; people's personal cultures keep them stuck in ancient expectations, patterns, and prejudices.

I will never forget my wife and I meeting a woman one day in church whom we would identify as a true Charlestonian. A Charlestonian is one whose family are longtime residents of this Southern city. The conversation somehow turned to the growing and important population of African-Americans in the community and the need to reach out in ministry and she instantly made some inappropriate remark thinking it was somehow funny. The confused look on our faces undoubtedly caused her to quickly change the topic. She was obviously an entrenched racist who was stuck in cultural bigotry. Is there a way forward? Nicodemus is the illustration that the answer is yes.

Stuck In Financial Bondage:
Zacchaeus (Luke 19:1–10)

We were taught a song in Sunday School class concerning Zacchaeus being "a wee little man" who climbed up into the sycamore tree to catch a glimpse of Jesus. It is a notable account because Zacchaeus was an embezzling, cheating tax collector for whom the people held great contempt. Zacchaeus was a man stuck in his greed, in his insatiable need for more money. There is no mention of wife or children in the account, which simply makes me pause to speculate whether money had become his ultimate passion. Perhaps his passion for wealth and riches had caused his relationships to break or be dysfunctional. How many people with great bank accounts are still stuck in their greed and lack of integrity? Wonderfully, the story ends in a true conversion and Jesus releases Zacchaeus from being stuck in this deception.

I have learned through the years that it is not simply the wealthy who find themselves stuck with greed and the need for riches. Greed at its root is simply the unnatural need to hoard and the never-ending desire for more. God is not against prosperity. There are too many scriptures that speak to His delight in seeing His people prosper. However, when the riches become the goal, then something is array. In fact, people from every economic status have been subject to getting stuck at this point.

Stuck In Disappointment:
Lazarus (John 11:1–44)

Lazarus was a man who died before his time in the opinion of his sisters, Mary and Martha. Jesus literally called Lazarus forth from out of the grave in an incredible demonstration of resurrection power. I liken Lazarus to the man who is stuck believing that his dreams have died and that there is no longer a future. How many people are living physically at the moment but their dreams and vision of a future have died on the inside?

Jesus majors in the resurrecting of dreams and purposes. He has the ability to step into an impossible situation and do something amazing in the midst of it. I have no idea what Lazarus did after coming forth out of the grave. I suspect the picture that was originally envisioned before his death was significantly modified after his resurrection. The point is that Jesus can unwrap the death cloth of feeling stuck and release you into a greater future.

Stuck In Various Bondages:
The Israelites (numerous Old Testament passages)

There may be no greater illustration of a people being stuck than the ancient Israelites in Egypt and their many other historical captivities. The bondages may have been precipitated by their own disobedience, but even those moments are not beyond God's mercy and redemption if we call to Him. I liken these ancient bondages to those stuck today in various addictions and strongholds feeling that they have no way out.

The Israelites also illustrate those who are stuck in dead-end employment and unjust circumstances. Their captivities and slavery directly speak to the feelings of being abused, taken advantage of, or getting the proverbial short end of the stick.

Invariably, someone who needs to read what I am about to write will pick up this book and read this line: *There is hope for you to get unstuck.* You can move forward. It can legitimately begin today.

Our nation is a country beset by personal addictions, strongholds, and bondages. People are literally spinning their internal wheels in their homes trying to break free but have reached the brink of exhaustion and resigned themselves to remaining stuck. You can be loosed, like ancient Israel was delivered and loosed, but it will take carefully and thoroughly walking a path that I will outline in this book.

Early in my ministry I committed one day a week to an urban rescue mission that focused on helping young men addicted to crack cocaine break free from the cycle of destruction and pain. Most of them had lost untold numbers of jobs and relationships. To be honest, if any relationships were intact, they were being held together by a thread. The addiction and the bondages were so severe in most of them that they had literally cemented themselves in a spot that would take a miracle to see them set free.

My primary job was to be their spiritual teacher and resource person. I met with them twice a week for a couple of hours in a classroom setting. It was strategized that for these young men to be assimilated back into a "normal" routine, they needed lots of structure and not simply a couch to fall asleep on during the teaching. Anyone who knows me understands that I have an anointing for teaching that calls the listener to stretch and enlarge. I am told that my vocabulary can at times eclipse most people's internal dictionaries. I am not intentionally trying to use big or unfamiliar words, but honestly I love to read, and that discipline has enlarged me, and it just spills out much of the time.

The problem in this context was that most of these young men had barely graduated from high school, if at all. Their education was minimal and what was retained had been lost long ago by the drugs and the street chatter, so it was a challenge for all of us to get on the same page. On a couple of occasions the group would chime out that my instruction was over their head. Was there any way I could make the material more elementary? I thought initially that I might have to do that, but then something arose in me and I said to the class, "No, I will not dumb down this material. I will not disrespect you as others have by treating you as kindergarteners. You are intelligent men who have the ability to understand what I am saying if you want to. The facts are, if you succeed in breaking free from your addictions and being released from this program, this vocabulary is the vocabulary of the successful and the economically accomplished. I expect no less from each one of you and I will treat you as my equals and you will rise to a new level instead of expecting me to sink to your level." They sat there silent. I don't think they had ever heard such a thing before.

During this time I noticed two distinct dynamics. First, every addict without fail would be challenged to "bolt" (this was the word used for a non-approved departure) the program at about the six-month mark. The men would tell me that the cocaine addiction would begin to "speak to them at night" and call them back to the streets. They said the pull to leave was incredible and difficult to explain, but each one attested that he had heard the voice. It was not unusual for me to come to class and see an empty chair and ask, "Where is so and so?" The guys would respond, "He heard the voice."

Second, those who resisted the temptation to go back into the same quagmire had a relentless perseverance to be free and apprehend a different future. They understood that they were paralyzed by this bondage, and they were ready to find a way out. I learned something extremely significant those days at the rescue mission: You can move forward if you want to, but there will always be voices calling you back.

The story would not be complete without my adding that I was able to watch scores of these young men graduate and be released to productive lives. I always chuckle concerning what happened at one graduation. In order to demonstrate their appreciation, the class bought me a nice Oakland A's baseball cap. It was a nice hat and I expressed my appreciation. The next week one of the leaders of that class dropped by and needed to confess something to me. He said, "Rev [that's what they called me], I wanted to let you know that the hat we got for you—well—one of guys stole it."

"You're kidding!" I responded.

"No," he said, "We didn't have the money initially, so to get it we had to lift it."

"So I'm wearing a 'hot' hat?" I asked.

"Not now," he responded. "We got it paid for this week and everything is cool, but we thought you needed to know."

I'm not sure I approve of how the story of the hat shook out, but I appreciate the perseverance of the group to start doing things right. If those young men could do it, I can assure the reader, you can do it too.

The point of this chapter is that it all begins by understanding that you are stuck and it's time to move forward. This isn't just psychological self-help stuff, but the Bible is going to give us insight and direction through the lives of numerous characters as to how that happens. I mentioned only a few of those characters in the list above, but I can almost guarantee you that whatever has ground you to a halt, there is a story, a precept, or a character in the Scriptures that addresses your situation. It's going to take work. It's going to take stepping up to another level and not expecting everyone to descend into your ditch. It's going to take ignoring the voices that are talking to you both internally and externally. Keep reading, my friend. Your answer is coming shortly. You can do this.

Chapter Two

Why Me?

It is a remarkable feature of humanity that when faced with a seemingly unexplainable moment, the question arises: "Why me?" It's as if there is a built-in mechanism in the psyche that instantly thinks in moments of challenge that such things should never happen to someone like you or me.

Philosophers have aptly called this consternation "The problem of evil." It simply poses the question that if God is omniscient (all-knowing), omnipotent (all-powerful), loving, and kind, then why does He not intervene in difficult moments, especially if those moments are horrific by any sensible standard? Why would God seemingly sit on the sidelines in our difficult seasons and at best "allow" such things to take place in our lives? Why would He allow injustice, unfairness, and the current quagmire of immovability in our life? Why would He seemingly sit idly by and allow His people to face unexplainable evil?

We say to ourselves, if not out loud then to those who may listen, "Why would God let this situation exist and continue in my life?" Everyone has heard the most relevant critique of the atheists when they ask a Christian, "Why do bad things happen to good people?" When you are stuck, you may not say it with the same sneer as your atheist friend, but inside you being to wonder: *Why me?*

In my years of pastoring I have had the opportunity to walk with people through particularly difficult moments. I have consoled the wife whose husband had broken trust through his infidelity. I have hugged the shoulders of parents who had lost children through either miscarriage or some birthing challenge. I have prayed for scores of people who had been fired or laid off from their employer unexpectedly. I have been in a living room when military aides knocked at the door to tell a young wife and mother that her husband had been killed in battle.

On one particularly difficult Sunday, my wife and I enjoyed lunch with a solid Christian couple in their mid-twenties. At lunch we laughed, shared, and spoke of all the possibilities this young family had for their future both in the church and their vocations. We spent an inordinately long time in conversation, which was uplifting, but eventually the time came to hug, kiss their babies good-bye, and go our separate ways until we could catch up the next Sunday. We had only been home about two hours when the phone rang. Tracie answered and the young wife screamed, "He's dead! He's dead!" As we jumped in the car headed to their home, the tragic afternoon story unfolded on the phone. This caring young man had gone straight over to help move some heavy equipment for his mother-in-law right after lunch. He called his young wife to tell her that he was on his way home with severe chest pains. As he walked in the door, he collapsed on the floor—unconscious.

The ambulance was called, and my wife and I arrived just as the paramedics were putting him into the ambulance. I listened as the senior paramedic carefully worded his statement to this young wife about taking her husband to the nearest emergency room. As the three of us jumped into our car following the ambulance, I listened as this young wife spoke, prayed, and believed all the things Christians say and do when tragedy is impending. She had two very young children—one was a baby, who needed a father—and she needed her husband.

We ran into the emergency room and she ran straight to the area where her husband was being treated. It was just a minute or two when we heard the ear-shattering scream from the waiting room as she was given the news that her husband had died of a massive coronary heart attack. I ran into the room and literally laid on top of this young man, whom I had just had lunch with a few hours earlier, and called out to God to raise him from the dead. We cried out for healing. We called life back into his mortal body. We appealed to the God of heaven to raise this man back to life. But there was no miracle on this occasion. As you might surmise, this young wife and mother was intensely distraught. In fact, by her own words and testimony years later, she would share how that moment put her in a spiral and quagmire of emotions that caused her to be stuck for years. If anyone had a reason, she had a legitimate reason to ask, "Why me?"

Undoubtedly you have reasons for asking that same question. I have found that it is difficult to measure each person's tragic moment with another's because each is personal and therefore it becomes massively significant. I am sure that if there were some cosmic referee or judge whose sole duty was to rate challenging situations based on their significance and pain, we all would feel some of ours would certainly be at the top of the list— when truth be told, as well as objectivity being exercised, there are people who have probably experienced pain far deeper than our own. The problem is, of course, that when we are in the midst of one of those moments it is hard to see past the personal nature of it all. We say, "Why me?" along with those whose questions are far more profound.

❖ ❖ ❖

It is important that we address the practical, philosophical question of "Why me?" The easiest answer might simply be "Why not?"

However, before we explore some of the reasons you might find yourself stuck, it is important that we address the practical, philosophical question of "Why me?" The easiest answer might simply be "Why not?" What makes us think we can simply escape life as it unfolds? And yet as Christian believers, we know that doesn't always help the moment. We don't like the arbitrary and capricious nature of that answer that somehow we are a part of the unlucky group who get targeted for tough circumstances. Surely serving God and living righteously afford some kind of force field that immunizes us from challenges. Sadly, that may be erroneously taught in some Christian circles or perhaps assumed, but it is poor theology.

Let's take a look at the question "Why bad things happen to good people?" There is a presupposition that exists behind the question that needs exposing. The question assumes that the world and its inhabitants are "good," and that "bad" moments are the intruders to what should be a relatively good life. In other words, life should generally be a nice place to navigate unless something I don't want, need, or expect gets dropped on me. I wish that were so.

The Scriptures tell us several things that actually make the question of "why bad things happen to good people" a fallacy.

As it is written: There is none righteous, no, not one. (Romans 3:10)

Through one man sin entered the world, and death through sin, and thus death spread to all men, because all sinned. (Romans 5:12)

Behold, I was brought forth in iniquity, And in sin my mother conceived me. (Psalm 51:5)

We are all like an unclean thing, And all our righteousnesses are like filthy rags; We all fade as a leaf, And our iniquities, like the wind, Have taken us away. (Isaiah 64:6)

The heart is deceitful above all things, And desperately wicked; Who can know it? (Jeremiah 17:9)

These references are but a few that underscore an incredibly important and foundational point in untangling our "stuck" moments.

First, the world is not by nature a "good" place, and similarly we by nature are not a "good" people. Why is this important? Because "bad" is not the intruder that trips into our otherwise "good" lives. In fact, biblically speaking, "bad" is the norm. To believe otherwise is to ignore what theologians refer to as the doctrine of depravity. We are unrighteous by nature and the creation is fallen through sin, which is why we need a Savior and why redemption is critical. To believe otherwise undermines the whole mission of Jesus and ostensibly causes us to be universalists (the heresy that states that everyone is "saved" no matter what).

Years ago I worked a second shift custodial job in order to put myself through graduate school and pay the bills. On one occasion the elementary school where I worked had engaged a young storyteller to entertain the children in an unexpected school assembly. He was incredibly gifted and charismatic when it came to storytelling and it just so happened that after the day's assembly he was waiting on his honorarium check in the gymnasium shooting baskets, and we began a conversation. He confidently explained to me that he believed humanity was basically good and that it just needed inspiration and encouragement to aspire to this "better self"—hence his work with children to build on this inherently "good" nature. I chuckled and said, "You obviously haven't been around schools much or watched the nightly news."

He responded incredulously, "What do you mean? I think I'm fairly knowledgeable about both of those subjects."

I said, "No offense, but have you watched kids and their natures? Have you seen the news being reported around the world? To believe the world and people are naturally 'good' by nature is a willful suspension of reality. Kids practice selfishness by nature and this world practices evil continually."

Of course, as the man was confronted with easily supplied illustrations to the contrary, the conversation shifted to a different subject, but the point was made. In our current state the world is groaning under the weight of unrighteousness, and evil and "bad" should be our normal expectation.

But wait! Life isn't bad at all times. In fact, there are times and seasons when life can be most enjoyable and in effect not only good but great. How do you reconcile these happenings and moments? By turning the initial question around and asking the more biblical question, "Why do good things happen to any of us?"

> Every good gift and every perfect gift is from above, and comes down from the Father of lights, with whom there is no variation or shadow of turning. (James 1:17)

So, what do we see? We see that bad is no longer the intruder upon a good people, but rather a good God intervenes in many amazing and profound ways, constantly, in an evil world among a sinful people. Why is that important? Because we never seem to ask the question, "Why me?" when we receive a blessing. We never seem to be too consternated over the fact that we are the one who gets a job, a promotion, or a raise. We never seem too surprised over the unusual check in the mail, the rebate, or a gift. We will say the obligatory "Praise the Lord" if we receive an inheritance, find money that was lost, or some debt cancellation takes place; but we rarely lose sleep over these blessings as we do when the challenges come our way.

We have come to expect modern medicine to cure all our diseases and take away all our pains, so when it does, we give the Lord a "hat tip" but rarely get too emotional over the blessing. Why is knowing this

> We see that bad is no longer the intruder upon a good people, but rather a good God intervenes in many amazing and profound ways, constantly, in an evil world among a sinful people.

important? First, it brings perspective to our difficult moments when we realize that most of us have already been recipients of some amazing blessings. Second, we are reminded that none of us can escape the fallenness of this present world and its inhabitants. When a bad situation presents itself, it is a reminder that for a time we all are stuck in a broken world.

However, even with the knowledge of how broken this world and people really are, it still does not personally address the moment of "Why me?" M. Scott Peck in his book *The Road Less Traveled* states:

> Storms may sweep down upon us from different directions and for different reasons. Sometimes Satan causes the storm. Sometimes people cause the storm. Sometimes I cause the storm. And sometimes the Lord sends the storm. But no matter who or what the cause, they all work to reveal some things.

So to answer the question "Why me?" it is critical to identify what kind of "stuck" you might find yourself in. We will explore more fully that question in the following chapters, but it is important to parse your sinkhole of a circumstance accurately, for what was meant to potentially help you can ultimately sink you without proper discernment.

Some may remember the old movies that would play on television weekend afternoons in the 1960s and 1970s. Several were serial movies—the Tarzan movies were some of my favorites. Somewhere in every Tarzan movie a man would find himself in quicksand. Quicksand looks to be a patch of solid ground in the jungle that when stepped on turns out to have the consistency of cold oatmeal. The unlucky victim started sinking down into the muck, only to find that struggling made it worse. Unless there was a vine to grab hold of, the victim disappeared without a trace (except perhaps the lone hat floating sadly on the surface). It was one of the greatest hazards of the jungle, and Tarzan saved more than a few from its murky clutches.

"Stuck" moments need to be evaluated, as to whether this "sand" of a circumstance is simply a brief pause that you will be easily freed from once the right evaluations are made and implemented; or is this "stuck" moment a "quicksand" that will engulf you the more you struggle and resist its glue-like substance? Many a person has been destroyed because they did not rightly evaluate and did not effectively handle the "stuck" moment. In fact, much like the person stuck in the quicksand of a Tarzan movie, you can identify a "stuck" person by listening to the sounds they make when in such a predicament.

The Sounds Of Cynicism

Cynicism is seen when a person becomes jaded in their emotions and beliefs to the point there is a deeply engrained distrust, disbelief, incredulity, and doubt concerning people and their personal future. Cynicism says things like "God can't be trusted," "God has His favorites and I'm not one of them," or "This will never change, and nobody really cares." Cynicism always thinks the worst and has a hard time ever seeing the good or the possibilities in any circumstance. Cynicism isn't a simple emotional glitch that momentarily forgets greater purposes; rather, it is a perspective and worldview whose foundation is total doubt.

The Sounds Of Disappointment

Disappointment is the foundation of bitterness. Bitter people are hurt and angry by what they feel life or people have dealt them. They are perpetually negative and refuse to release grudges or exercise forgiveness. They are jealous and notorious pouters because they constantly feel as if they have been treated unfairly or unjustly.

In our modern, online era, the sounds of disappointment are regularly shared through social media and blog sites. There is a generation whose transparency and disappointment have merged, and they let the world know.

The Sounds Of Self-Pity

People exercising self-pity want to be seen as the victims. They actually enjoy people seeing them as pathetic. It is usually accompanied by a depression and overwhelming sense of gloom concerning their lives at the moment. This is the theme of almost every conversation. All sense of joy has been drained out of those who practice self-pity.

The Sounds Of Excuses

Those who offer excuses may be blame-shifters as well, depending on the depth of their excuses. Their situations are, however, not their fault and everyone needs to know that whatever their current paralyzing circumstances may be, there is someone or something else to blame. They would not be where they are had it not been for someone or something doing this to them.

The Sounds Of Regrets

Those who harbor regret constantly wish they could go back and relive most of their lives. They are paralyzed by what has happened and are convinced that if they could have a "do-over" it would have turned out differently. There is always much whining and pining over the past, which clouds any discussion or vision concerning the future.

Perhaps you have been a "Why me?" kind of person. Perhaps the sounds listed above have been some of the sounds emanating from your life. This is not a point of judgment or condemnation but rather an opportunity to recognize yourself as being stuck and needing some help finding your way out. No one, most of all me, would minimize the current circumstance you might find yourself in. It is your personal paralysis and it is the issue at hand. The only failure at this point is to dodge this moment of identification by saying, "Not me." Don't allow this moment or your circumstances to become your quicksand. Press through your reading and let's nail down what exactly is going on.

Chapter Three

◆◆◆

The God-Ordained "Stuck"

Not every "stuck" moment is due to a poor decision or the work of the devil. As we will explore shortly, those dynamics can be at work. However, before we leap to those situations, it might be best to explore those "stuck" moments that God has designed for His specific purposes.

Sometimes God intentionally closes every possible door before you in order that He might forge a greater work through you and accomplish a purpose beyond your current understanding of the situation. Such was the familiar story of Joseph (Genesis 37–50), which covers an inordinately large space of writing in the totality of Scripture. Fourteen total chapters, not counting other references in other books, are used to tell the story of this immature young man who becomes a global influencer. If you do not know

> ◆◆◆
>
> Sometimes God intentionally closes every possible door before you in order that He might forge a greater work through you.

the story of Joseph, I would encourage you to take the time to read it. It is an important illustration of understanding God's ways.

A young boy is given a remarkable dream of rulership and

influence only to find himself sold into slavery by his jealous brothers, falsely accused by a seductive woman, sent to prison for a crime he didn't commit, and ultimately forgotten by a chief butler who said he would put in a good word for him. Joseph's situation is the classic illustration of a person being stuck in a circumstance with seemingly no way out. Yet God in His strange and remarkable ways creates a scenario in which Joseph is summoned from prison to interpret Pharaoh's dreams and the story makes a 180-degree turn. Joseph finds favor and is installed as the number-two leader in all of Egypt. When his brothers are made aware of Joseph's new status, he interprets the events for them by saying:

> So now it was not you who sent me here, but God. (Genesis 45:8)

> As for you, you meant evil against me; but God meant it for good, in order to bring it about as it is this day, to save many people alive. (Genesis 50:20)

This is what I have defined as a "God-ordained 'stuck.'" You are where you are because God has orchestrated and designed a path for you to walk, which will lead to His good purpose, which you cannot see or understand at the moment. It may appear twisted, convoluted, unjust, unfair, and even frustrating; but the Lord uses these moments for numerous purposes in the economy of His will.

Shortly after receiving Christ as my Lord and Savior, I was called to preach and began my training for vocational ministry. The first couple of years of training I found amazing and unprecedented favor with regard to open doors to speak and minister. I was invited to preach at churches and events far beyond the normal opportunities of a young rookie preacher. It was an amazing and humbling time as God demonstrated His ability to open incredible doors of ministry.

In the midst of that favorable season, I was engaged to be married and I desired to continue my education, so I needed some structure and consistent resources to achieve those goals. As noted earlier, I was able to secure a custodial job at an elementary school, with hours from 3:00 pm to 11:00 pm. This job paid surprisingly well and provided the hours and flexibility to go to graduate school and study. Obviously the ministry opportunities I once enjoyed were put on the backburner to fulfill these other important responsibilities. Please bear with me at this point as I need to share some details in order for you to connect with what would become a three-year "stuck" season.

An evening custodian's primary responsibility is to clean up the building for the next day's use. I would arrive at 3:00 pm to begin shortly before school dismissed at 3:30 pm. In that 30 minutes I would be able to organize the evening cleaning and get a head start on what needed to be done. Custodial and maintenance work should be esteemed by everyone because although it is behind the scenes and appears simple and menial, without it the general atmosphere for instruction would be greatly impaired. The sad fact is, however, that in many instances these service people are treated shabbily and are assumed to be of few skills— for why else would anyone "choose" to be a custodian?

I found this to be partially true as students, parents, teachers, and administrators tended to treat me as one who might possibly be mentally or developmentally challenged. Teachers would talk unusually slowly to me, believing I could understand at best only two-syllable words spoken deliberately despite the fact I was fluent in Greek and had a working knowledge of Hebrew, Latin, and German. The kids, especially the boys, would do gross and disgusting things in the bathroom, knowing full well they were leaving it for me to clean up.

I became convinced there was a maniacal demon assigned to that school who would make sure kids would get sick at their stomachs at 3:25 pm, causing them to vomit on the carpets rather than the tile. I would regularly find myself cleaning up such messes in the middle of the hallway at the exact time the dismissal bell would ring. The kids would swarm the hallway and provide elementary school commentary on the mess I was having to clean up.

It was more than humbling—it felt chronically demeaning. Imagine that for five days a week for three straight years. I wanted out more times than I could count, but the tension between my pride and my paycheck kept me at that elementary school cleaning toilets and sweeping floors. Many an evening my wife would drop by the school with dinner so we might eat together and see each other. Many of the conversations surrounded the topic of "how long" would I be imprisoned at this job and when God might open a new door that would be more. I wondered on more than one occasion if I had made the right decision taking this job. Sure, it fulfilled some needs to accomplish other goals, but the immobilization of those years was excruciating. My wife had the patience of a true saint as I would gripe and complain on a regular basis.

While all this was taking place there was another situation blossoming, which was camouflaged to my discernment for many months. My normal routine was to enter at 3:00 pm and go from room to room with a trash barrel on wheels to dump the wastepaper baskets of each individual classroom. Each room task only lasted about two minutes tops, but multiply that two minutes by five days a week and then again by three years and it becomes a significant amount of time spent with each teacher in every room. One of those teachers was a kindergarten teacher by the name of Mrs. Miller. She was old enough at that time to be my mom and almost every time I got to her room at the end of the day the class had deteriorated into a kindergarten circus. So, I would often walk into her room as she was yelling to gain control of the class and I would smile and whisper to her that she was "mean Mrs. Miller." The good-natured joking began an innocuous relationship which was about to become significantly different.

I walked into work one day and was told that Mrs. Miller had contracted a serious cancer. She had been hospitalized in order to begin testing and treatment for the disease. I knew she had no pastor and no real Christian faith, so I presumed that this was my moment to minister to her. I dressed up in coat and tie and headed to the hospital. Upon my arrival I saw that everyone who was an important someone in her life was visiting her that evening. She was receiving her teaching colleagues as well as top-level administrators from the school district. The room was crowded and when I entered she was pleasant and thanked me for coming, but it was obvious she would rather have the attention of the other significant people. After all, why visit with the custodian when you could have the attention of so many important people?

I excused myself and headed back to the elevator to leave. I will admit that I was irritated, perhaps embarrassed and aggravated, by my reception and snub, even though it was she who was in the challenging situation. I complained to God on the elevator ride down saying, "Okay, Lord—I did what You would want of me. I tried to reach out to her and was prepared to share the gospel, but obviously I wasn't that important to her. If she dies and goes to hell, it's not on me. I tried." I felt righteously satisfied. It was at that moment however, that the Holy Spirit put a direct impression upon me that was clear and unmistakable. I would use the phrase that the Lord "spoke" to me, but I am quite sure there was no audible voice. Nevertheless, the impression was undeniable and clear. It was as if He had audibly said, "This is your assignment. Don't undervalue this moment." It knocked the irritation right out of me. I felt now exponentially embarrassed and corrected by the Lord Himself. I said softly, "Okay, Sir," and what happened the next six months literally reshaped my thinking.

Cancer is a relentless and despicable enemy. It causes upheaval wherever it goes. Mrs. Miller began to manifest the symptoms of the disease. Her husband couldn't handle the pressure and responsibilities of being a caretaker and support. Sadly and unbelievably, he eventually left her in the middle of this fight. The celebrities and colleagues of the elementary school and school district slowly faded away to their own responsibilities and ceased coming to see her. The only one left to help her was the custodian. In the midst of her battle I was able to present the gospel, and gratefully she received Christ as her personal Savior. Unfortunately, her nascent faith and relentless pain made it difficult to share the possibilities of supernatural healing. In the end, all I was able to do was sit beside her on the porch, rocking back and forth, holding her hand while sharing thoughts about heaven.

I will never forget the day when I went to work, and the principal asked me to come into his office and he shared with me that Mrs. Miller had passed away the previous night. He said one of her last requests was that I would officiate her memorial service. It was to be held at the school gymnasium. This wasn't totally unexpected, and I agreed.

On the day of the memorial service my wife and I arrived at the school gymnasium to an overflow parking lot. Upon our entrance to the gym, we noticed the place filled to capacity and beyond. It was remarkable. Of course, her teaching colleagues along with her students and parents were in attendance, but so were all the district administration and superintendents on the front row. Students and parents from years gone by were in attendance as well. What I didn't know was that the local newspaper had been doing a story on her and two of their reporters were there, as well as reporters from the local television station. It was as if the whole town had gathered in that place and the irony hit me when I realized that they had come to honor her and ironically hear the custodian.

You might ask, "What did you say?" I decided that since this might be my one and only shot to witness to the entire school district, I would simply go for it. It's amazing what you will do when you feel you have nothing to lose. I spoke like a man preaching his last sermon to a dying people. The response was remarkable. All of a sudden this obscure custodian was front and center.

The influence that followed that memorial service was little short of miraculous. The district superintendent gave me an open-door status with him any time I wanted it. Parents would follow me around the school during work hours while I was picking up the trash, seeking my advice. My school mailbox was filled with requests to know more about Jesus and the Christian faith. Beyond that, the newspaper and the television station released stories about Mrs. Miller and the custodian who did her funeral service. People would recognize me around town and say, "Hey, aren't you that janitor they wrote about in the paper?" I had become quite paradoxically the celebrity custodian, and while that was amusing, the more important thing I learned was that there are times God causes you to be stuck in order to accomplish His greater purposes and learn His deeper lessons.

Charles Schultz, the creator of the Peanuts comic strip, once had Charlie Brown carefully building a sandcastle in the beach sand. Standing back to admire his work, he was soon engulfed by a downpour, which leveled the castle. Standing before the smooth place where his artwork once stood, he said, "There must be a lesson here, but I don't know what it is." How often do we feel like that when we are in a situation in which we feel stuck and immobilized and think that somehow God has forgotten us? What are the lessons? Let me suggest five lessons I learned from my experience and what you will learn from those moments when you are in a God-ordained "stuck."

You Will Learn To Grow In Faith And Patience.

How else might the Lord increase these two important features in your walk and life if you do not face the feelings of immobilization? If a person prays for patience, it should really be unsurprising that you might be put in situations where it must be exercised. Every scriptural virtue is mere theory unless you are put into circumstances that demand that they be manifested through your life. God is committed to His people walking out those character traits that will bring them into greater maturity.

> Every scriptural virtue is mere theory unless you are put into circumstances that demand that they be manifested through your life.

Your Motives And Attitudes Will Be Purified.

If most of us were honest we would have to admit that our motives and attitudes need work. We whine and gripe far too easily at times.

We serve in much the same way that politicians "serve" by craving spotlights and visibility. "Stuck" places are usually obscure places that provide the best environment to refine these aspects of our life. Your "stuck" place is a place of important revelation that can pinpoint things that need to be addressed.

You Will Demonstrate To God Faithfulness To A Task.

The great celestial greeting we all should yearn to hear as we enter the presence of the Lord upon our death is "Well done, good and faithful servant." Ultimately what impresses God is not your skills, talent, or even gifts but rather your faithfulness to the moments and circumstances He places you in. For me, as remarkable as all my previous preaching assignments may have been in those early years, the real test was my faithfulness to a kindergarten teacher who was battling cancer in a place no one could see. Your real test may be at this very moment in your obscure, "stuck" place. Don't minimize your current moment.

You Will Become More Teachable.

When you've done everything you know to do and you are still stuck, you are left with a short list of options. You can quit and throw in the towel or become teachable and learn what you may not know. In the earlier reference to Joseph, one can easily pinpoint the fact that this young man with a quick mouth had to learn how to measure his words and exercise forgiveness. Every immobilization, every frustration, every unsolicited circumstance is a teachable moment for future reference. I made the decision years ago that wherever I may find myself and whatever may be happening to me, there is something I can learn and be wiser. Don't miss those lessons of being stuck.

You Will Consecrate Yourself To His Will.

C. S. Lewis writes, "God will not have a part of us. He will only have us if He can have all of us. If we claim we have given all of ourselves to God and are still holding back on one or two areas, we are only fooling ourselves. We need to start over with our gift to Him and this time make it complete."

Your God-ordained "stuck" moment is actually an altar of consecration if you can see it clearly. These moments are the ones when, as the nineteenth-century Holiness writers would say, you "die to yourself" and embrace the full will of God for your life. What real choice do you have? You can perpetually strive against the circumstances you find yourself in, or you can consecrate yourself to the purposes of God and enjoy the inner peace that comes when you know you are in the center of His will.

> ❖ ❖ ❖
>
> Your God-ordained "stuck" moment is actually an altar of consecration if you can see it clearly.

Victor Frankl, the great Viennese psychoanalyst and Holocaust survivor, once said, *What is to give light must endure burning.* You and I are called to be the "light of the world." That light shines most brightly in adverse and dark moments. Frankl is right to use the analogy of burning as these "stuck" moments incinerate what is unlike Jesus and prepare us for the mission ahead. So as you are evaluating and discerning your particular circumstances of being stuck, make sure you factor in the distinct possibility that God has orchestrated your steps for this moment.

Chapter Four

❖·❖·❖

The Demonically-Orchestrated "Stuck"

There is no question that the enemy (Satan) can, for a variety of reasons, cause you to be stuck and immobilized. Of course, as believers we have been given all power and authority necessary to rebuke and bind his activity and schemes as well as scatter his tactics and strategies (Ephesians 6:10–18). That being said, it is important to distinguish who and what is causing this situation you now find yourself in. Is it God or is it the devil?

Sometimes you can discern the answer quickly while at other moments it may take time. Our first response cannot be to instantly do spiritual warfare when in fact we may be where we are in the will of God; yet at the same time we are not required to be the devil's doormat and passively endure an attack or detour. These moments of being stuck can be tricky indeed. Unfortunately, many Christians do not pray and discern their "stuck" moments before automatically assuming that this challenge they are facing absolutely must be the devil. We

❖·❖·❖

As sophisticated as we Americans think we are at times, it is fascinating to note how undiscerning and spiritually gullible we can be.

are living in an era in which the sum total of our theology fits on the back bumper of our cars. A five-to-seven-word Christian bumper sticker with a pithy saying rarely encapsulates the whole counsel of Scripture. As sophisticated as we Americans think we are at times, it is fascinating to note how undiscerning and spiritually gullible we can be.

It is true foundationally that God is good and the devil is bad. It is true that Jesus came to give us "abundant life" and the devil seeks "to steal, and to kill, and to destroy" (John 10:10). These things are important elementary truths. However, these truths are most often tied to final outcomes of situations and not necessarily the nature of the journey, process, or circumstances of getting there. In other words, every believer may walk through difficult seasons (Ecclesiastes 3:1–8) that are appointed by God for a beautiful purpose (Ecclesiastes 3:11). Paul reaffirms this principle by stating,

> We know that all things work together for good to those who love God, to those who are called according to His purpose. (Romans 8:28)

The literal Greek supports the translation, which can actually read, "God *causes* all things to work together for good..." The Lord can be involved in the most desperate of situations and most certainly in the midst of your immobilization, *causing* an important outcome. God's "good" is not always defined by the convenience, ease, and comfort we may be feeling at the moment. The Christian life ultimately is a consummating journey to an eternal place and reward, not necessarily a challenge-free, temporal existence. I remind the reader concerning this truth because there is a tension and mystery at times as we walk with God concerning His sovereignty over our circumstances and the interruption of demonic influence or poor decision-making. In other words, make sure you aren't rebuking a purposeful, divine season. Yes, this will take great discernment, prayer, and maturity to distinguish.

That being said, it is still possible that a demonic attack has targeted your life.

It is never a good thing to give too much time or credence to our adversary; however, understanding his strategies and tactics can better prepare us for those moments of battle and attack. I have come to believe that Satan's first strategy in all of our lives is to blind us from the truth of the gospel and the good news of redemption (2 Corinthians 4:4). For many, including me, church attendance does not necessarily assure that one is illuminated to their need of salvation. Satan's schemes to "blind" people are remarkable and effective. This is why Paul prayed,

> That the God of our Lord Jesus Christ, the Father of glory, may give to you the spirit of wisdom and revelation in the knowledge of Him, the eyes of your understanding being enlightened; that you may know what is the hope of His calling, what are the riches of the glory of His inheritance in the saints, and what is the exceeding greatness of His power toward us who believe, according to the working of His mighty power which He worked in Christ when He raised Him from the dead and seated Him at His right hand in the heavenly places, far above all principality and power and might and dominion, and every name that is named, not only in this age but also in that which is to come. (Ephesians 1:17–21)

If his first strategy fails and the person receives Christ as Savior, then this relentless adversary turns to plan B. This second strategy is to do everything possible to frustrate, even detour, the plans and purposes of God in the life of the believer. Now while it is true that there is no comparison between God (the infinite, uncreated, all-powerful One, who has always been and shall forever be) and the devil (a finite, created, fallen angel), it is beyond dispute that Satan can get his fingers, through his demonic forces, into our lives and circumstances.

For we do not wrestle against flesh and blood, but against principalities, against powers, against the rulers of the darkness of this age, against spiritual hosts of wickedness in the heavenly places. (Ephesians 6:12)

For though we walk in the flesh, we do not war according to the flesh. For the weapons of our warfare are not carnal but mighty in God for pulling down strongholds, casting down arguments and every high thing that exalts itself against the knowledge of God, bringing every thought into captivity to the obedience of Christ. (2 Corinthians 10:3–5)

One of the keys, it appears, in discerning a legitimate demonic immobilization is the presence of a blatant hostility to the revealed will of God.

The story is told of famous Russian dissident Alexander Solzhenitsyn. He was a prisoner for years in the Soviet Gulag, working in fields through backbreaking labor and slow starvation. One day the hopelessness became too much to bear. He felt no purpose in fighting on or that his life would have any ultimate purpose. Laying his shovel down one day, he slowly walked to a bench in which to sit and rest. He knew the price of this kind of act. He knew that a guard at any moment would order him to rise and when he failed to do so would beat him to death with his own shovel. This was a routine scene in the Gulag.

As Solzhenitsyn sat waiting, he felt a presence next to him. It was an old man with a wrinkled face. Hunched over, the man, with a stick in his hand, drew at Solzhenitsyn's feet the sign of the cross. As Solzhenitsyn stared at the cross, his entire perspective shifted. He knew he was merely one man against the powerful Soviet empire. He understood the evil that was thrust upon him. Yet at that moment he also knew that the hope of all humanity was represented in that cross, and through its power anything was possible. He arose, picked up his shovel, and went back to work.

Your situation may not be a Soviet Gulag, but discerning believers can recognize those moments when evil is thrust upon them for seemingly no reason besides their faith and convictions.

I will never forget one summer evening in my late teen years, staying after working hours on a Friday to do some engine work on my car in the parking lot. I had a revival meeting to drive to that weekend and I needed the car to be in good condition. My employer had the tools I needed to adjust some things in my car's engine, so I stayed alone after hours to get it done quickly.

Next door to the company I worked for was a fence company with whom we shared the parking lot. On Fridays, after working late, their employees would make their weekly end-of-the-week "beer run." They would consistently every Friday come driving in at closing time shouting and hollering on the back of a large truck, indicating that the weekend had already started and the alcohol was flowing freely. One of them, who coincidentally I attended high school with, saw me under the hood working on my vehicle and from a distance offered me a beer as he slowly walked his way toward me. I'm a non-drinker by conviction, so I smiled and politely declined the offer, which evidently was perceived as a grave offense. I guess he felt perhaps that I had embarrassed him before his friends. I honestly did not know why his mood suddenly changed except due to his obvious inebriation.

He continued walking across the parking lot toward me, apparently wanting to start a fight. He said he wanted to kick my tail (not exactly using that vocabulary) because of the perceived slight. What was I to do? I didn't ask for this moment. I was minding my own business. God was obviously not a part of the dynamics of the moment. I could not in that instant see a teachable moment.

Do I fight?

Do I turn the other cheek?

What about the weekend revival meeting?

Do I go into those services with two black eyes?

Do I teach on the biblical principle of self-defense?

Do I practice self-defense?

This moment is what a demonic attack most often times looks like. It brings confusion, convolution, and potential detouring of the plans of God. What did I do in this situation? In this instance I shared with a soft response a brief testimony of my faith in Jesus Christ and His personal commands and convictions upon my life that I abstain from such participation. All I knew to do was invoke the name of Jesus and believe for the best. This young man suddenly appeared embarrassed. His hostility began to subside. He looked chagrined and simply mumbled a contrite "Sorry," patted my cheeks in an affectionate way, and went back to his party.

Demonically-orchestrated immobilization tends to take on this type of look. There is a sense of the enemy's fingers in it through one's discernment. While Satan and his demons are spirits, they most often use the lives of oppressed people, unknowingly on many occasions, to do their work of drama, detours, and destruction. These moments are most often unsolicited and a surprise. The key is that the target is not simply to frustrate and harm you as the believer but the plan and purposes of God that are being expressed and manifested in your life. There are no lessons, personal refinement, or spiritual consecration at work. A demonic immobilization is a complete and unsolicited attack and collapse on the will of God in your life.

> ❖ ❖ ❖
>
> **Immobilizing circumstances must be recognized at both the natural and spiritual level.**

I have walked through enough "stuck" moments to be able to say that these situations have a different ferocity surrounding them. I know that many may be reading this at this moment and thinking that distinguishing the type of "stuck" you are facing seems nebulous and elusive. I understand and can sympathize to some degree. Spiritual attacks are spiritually appraised and discerned. Your Christian walk is not simply the stoic implementation of principles and going through a multi-page checklist to evaluate the potential of a demonic attack, but rather it includes spiritually discerning the moment. Immobilizing circumstances must be recognized at both the natural and spiritual level.

I pastored for twenty-two years in Charleston, South Carolina. One of the infamous historical reputations of this city was a little-known fact that it put George Whitefield, the voice of the First Great Awakening, in a jail cell for several days. His incarceration stemmed from the fact that there were Anglican clergy who did not appreciate his ministry in what they considered "their" city. Therefore, some of the clergy concocted and fabricated false charges and were able to have him arrested. Whitefield, fortunately, had supporters and friends in the area and they were able to bail him out and get him out of town.

Interestingly, Charleston, while being known as "The Holy City," has had opportunity to experience all the notable historical awakenings and revivals that we now identify. Yet remarkably the city never seems to embrace those opportunities but rather finds ways to dismiss and avoid a legitimate revival from God. Why is this? Is Charleston as a city simply stuck in a challenging place or season? I rather think not. I believe there are demonic forces at work that have been surprisingly effective in maintaining the state of its spiritual immobilization. This is what happened to Whitefield as he responded to God's call to minister to this city.

Ironically, I, although I am no George Whitefield, have experienced the same sense of immobilization while ministering in that city. What about you? Have there been moments in your life, almost unexplainably, in which drama and destruction descended upon you without warning or apparent reason? Have there been moments in which circumstances have made a 180-degree detour without any plausible or understandable reason for it? Do you find yourself immobilized through no apparent decision of your own making and utterly contrary to the divine seasons you have walked in previous days? Then there is a high probability that you may be the recipient of some demonically-orchestrated schemes to immobilize you in the purposes of God.

It is important to you, the reader, to grasp this point. I can give example after example of a demonically-orchestrated immobilization, but it must be discerned in your own life and circumstances. This book does not have as a primary purpose the tools of spiritual warfare, but it cannot escape the possibility that warfare and demonic strategies may be involved. John Wimber wrote in his book *Power Evangelism* that the believer is not trying "to find a demon under every rock"; however, we must also understand that "when you turn over some rocks, they may indeed be there." C. S. Lewis said something similar when he wrote in his famous book *The Screwtape Letters*:

> There are two equal and opposite errors into which our race can fall about the devils. One is to disbelieve in their existence. The other is to believe, and to feel an excessive and unhealthy interest in them. They themselves are equally pleased by both errors and hail a materialist or a magician with the same delight.

If you are facing one of these moments, then arise and wage battle with your spiritual adversary. The precepts I will suggest in a later chapter can certainly be applied and implemented at this place, but an exercising of the believer's rights and authority against the works of the enemy must also be applied.

> And they overcame him [Satan] by the blood of the Lamb and by the word of their testimony, and they did not love their lives to the death. (Revelation 12:11, emphasis mine)

Satan is not rebuked by implementation of principles alone (although obedience is critical and not to be diminished). Rather, a confident and aggressive confession of scripture from one's own mouth concerning Christ's victory and Satan's defeat is essential. The power of

God's Word from your lips will act as "the sword of the Spirit" in these instances (Ephesians 6:17).

Chapter Five

The Self-Inflicted "Stuck"

I want to spend a little more time and space dealing with this third possibility of why you might be stuck in life. For many, ignorance, poor decision-making, and lack of self-awareness lead to immobilization and lack of forward movement. The Scriptures are full of admonishment and illustrations when it comes to our own ability to create our own messes. Literally the first story in the book of Genesis dealing with human beings is an account of a poor choice when both Adam and Eve make a bad decision and partake of the fruit of the forbidden tree (Genesis 3:6). Sadly, that scenario is played out innumerable times in all our lives. We are where we are because we made a poor decision, sometimes in the light of God trying to help us avoid that mistake.

Early in my ministry I received a call from a district superintendent in the denomination I was part of at that time to consider moving to a historic church in Oakland, California. I was in my mid-twenties, and to be asked to pastor such an important and prestigious church in the long history of our denomination at such a young age was considered an honor. The list of previous pastors of this local church read like the Who's Who of denominational superstars.

I realize that such thoughts should be foreign to the servant of the Lord, but in absolute transparent honesty, the invitation caused no small sense of self-importance. It also caused no small sense of spiritual deafness. At the time of the invitation, I was pastoring a church that was small and seemingly unimportant. The congregation was stuck in traditions and preferences that made the assignment super-challenging in my estimation. Added on top of all the ministry challenges, they had a poverty mentality that reflected on how we were compensated and cared for, and with a growing family with mouths to feed, that was no small issue. I was offended and irritated by that current assignment and was looking for some way out. I felt stuck, under-appreciated, and neglected. It is not a flattering picture I paint of myself, but it is an honest one.

My wife and I jumped onto a jet and flew to Oakland to visit with both the district superintendent and church board. They rolled out the red carpet and took us on a mind-numbing two-day tour of city and church that would dazzle any impressionable young minister and wife. The city of Oakland is directly across the bay from San Francisco, and the church rested in the hills of Oakland. What would be my office window, which was enormous, faced the distant city of San Francisco. At night the lights of the city, bridges, and ships were easily viewed, and the picture was incredible.

The church itself was historic, actually one of the original churches pastored by the founder of the denomination at the turn of the twentieth century. The facility was excellent, large, and well cared for. The leadership of the church was sharp and successful in their personal lives and endeavors. The church gave every indication of being healthy, wealthy, and poised for the future. The boardroom we met in looked like the typical Fortune 500 conference room.

My head was spinning, and I was grinning. After the meeting on the final evening, the district superintendent took us to the edge of the property, and as we gazed down the majestic hills of Oakland and looked across the expanse of water, lights, and bridges, he said, "Why wouldn't God be calling you to a place like this?" It was a closing worthy of a used car salesman. That was all it took for me, and at that moment before I uttered one single prayer to seek God's will concerning this matter, I had already made up my mind: "California, here we come." This was my destiny. This was my future of success. How could it not be the will of God to come to this place? After all, it was a promotion, it was financial increase, and it was an incredibly visible place for ministry and celebrity.

It would turn out to be one of the most devastating decisions of my life.

As I look back decades later, it is so easy to see where I made a bad decision. Hindsight is indeed 20/20, and my motives and misinterpretation of signs during that interview process are now so clear to me. I can point to numerous places along the way in that process and can see where signs and sounds were made by the Lord Himself to help me make the right decision, but I decided this was too important a position and moment for me to think it could be anything other than the perfect will of God. I was wrong.

I remember the last night we were in Oakland, staying at the district superintendent's house before giving him my final decision. I woke up in the middle of the night incredibly sick to my stomach. I did not have a propensity for nausea, so I assumed it was either something I had eaten or perhaps the devil trying to discourage me from coming to this assignment and he was trying to put a sickness upon me. I was sick multiple times that night, each time rebuking the enemy in what I thought was an attempt to steal "my heart's desire." I was going to pastor this church no matter what. My will was set. I may have prayed an obligatory prayer somewhere along the way to be able to say that I had "prayed about it," but again, I was full-steam ahead.

Tracie and I moved to Oakland and began the ministry at this particular church. About six weeks after getting settled in, we were stuck in our car in the famous Bay Area traffic nightmare. The setting was appropriate and ironic for the revelation that hit us both. It was at this moment that we looked at each other and almost simultaneously said out loud, "We have made a gigantic mistake." I realized that my sickness that night we spent at the district superintendent's house was not a demonic attack or even my hidden reluctance to do the will of God—but rather a manifestation of my spirit trying to tell me that this church was incredibly sick and that I needed to beware and in all likelihood stay away. But we had made the decision.

Truthfully, I alone had made the decision. This was a self-inflicted, bad decision that we were now stuck with. That "stuck" moment lasted for two years. It was excruciatingly painful at times. I begged God to deliver me from my mistake, but I sat in this "stuck" for two long years. We were thousands of miles away from any family support system. The church itself was incredibly out of order and replete with hidden sin and inequity. No one was interested in pursuing the purposes of God.

Did God "cause" some things to work together for good in that situation because we loved Him and were called to His purposes (Romans 8:28)? Of course—the Lord can maximize any twisted moment in His sovereignty for His glory. But that does not diminish the fact that I got into this predicament because of my own devices. This was not the devil's fault. This was not God exercising some maniacal, arbitrary, capricious plan to break me beyond my tolerance. It was the repercussion of my own bad decisions.

❖ ❖ ❖

I have no way to quantify by percentage the predominant ways people get stuck in life, but I am persuaded that a large percentage happen because of self-inflicted decisions.

Now this is the epiphany that many people need to receive. You may be in your "stuck" circumstance because you made a poor decision. It may be that your immobilization is a self-inflicted, bad decision that has ground your life seemingly to a halt. I'm not trying to increase any sense of remorse or embarrassment in your life. Remember—I have done exactly the same thing. What I am trying to do is to help you squeeze every ounce of understanding and revelation this moment can provide so you will avoid doing this again. I have no way to quantify by percentage the predominant ways people get stuck in life, but I am persuaded that a large percentage happen because of self-inflicted decisions.

What causes us to make these poor decisions? What is it that we succumb to that produces an environment in which we are stuck? I suppose there might be a hundred potential snares that can grind our life to a halt, but I want to explore what I consider to be the top seven in most people's lives.

We Are Offended.

Without a doubt or any scientific research to back up the claim, I am convinced that people who refuse to deal with offense will find themselves stuck on various levels. Offense creates bitterness and unforgiveness that consume the heart and mind. You cannot move forward because the event of the past that has caused the offense is redirecting your eyesight.

My wife tells the personal story of the months just following one of the greatest challenges of our lifetime, which was the navigation of a church split. It was an incredibly difficult time for both of us to forgive certain players who had caused such pain and had spread false stories and allegations. We each had our individual challenges in pressing through our offenses to forgiveness and freedom.

During this time we were trying to sell our house, which was on the island where our former church was located. We needed to close that chapter of our life and establish roots in the new area to which we would minister. We had a fantastic house in a desirable area, but it was as if it were secretly hidden and out of the plain sight of buyers. It was priced right, and my wife is a phenomenal decorator and marketer, so there was no natural reason that a buyer would not quickly snatch the house up, especially in the current seller's market. We literally sat on the house, stuck there, for eighteen months. The real estate agents were baffled. We were frustrated. What could be the hold-up in an otherwise "hot" market?

One day my wife was getting ready to go out and as she was completing the finishing touches on her make-up in front of the mirror, a thought entered her mind concerning a group of people who had spearheaded our ousting. The scripture came to mind concerning Jesus, while on the cross, uttering the words, "Father, forgive them, for they know not what they do" (Luke 23:34). My wife said to herself, "Ah, but I don't have to forgive them because they knew exactly what they were doing." (I wish she could tell the story because it is far more powerful than my writing.)

She then recounts: The room began to spin as if she were in a colorful time warp taking her back to an event almost two decades earlier at a previous church when she had harshly corrected a young girl in the youth group. In that moment of revelation, Tracie began to weep at how she had mishandled this young girl. She began to cry, "Lord, I didn't know what I was doing. Please forgive me."

The Holy Spirit responded to her by saying, "EXACTLY! Just like the people who unfairly treated you did not know what they were doing."

At that moment she received an epiphany, fell down on her knees in the bathroom, and one by one forgave every individual involved in the church split. In true transparency and genuineness, she released her offense and truly forgave them. Amazingly, only four days later, we had multiple offers on the house and sold it for five thousand dollars more than the original listing price. In this situation, dealing with the offense caused a release from this "stuck" moment.

Incidentally, my wife also reached out to the young girl she saw in her epiphany in order to reconnect and potentially reconcile with her. After locating the young girl and having a wonderful conversation with her, it was discovered that she had never held an offense towards Tracie. Though hundreds of miles apart, they have become social media friends and stay in touch on a regular basis—sharing each other's lives. The amazing work of the Holy Spirit in moments like these cannot be underestimated.

We Are Disillusioned.

Have you ever taken a moment in your life and looked around at where you were and what you were doing and said to yourself, "This isn't exactly the picture I had envisioned years ago as to where I would be at this point in my life?" Honestly, disillusionment tends to be the place of immobilization for so many middle-aged people. It is the breeding ground for the colloquial "mid-life crisis." It can also be the catalyst for being stuck for many who have experienced real or perceived disappointments in relationships, especially church life.

We Are Full Of Pride And Arrogance.

In two locations in Scripture we are told, "God resists the proud, but gives grace to the humble" (James 4:6; 1 Peter 5:5). For the Lord to declare something twice indicates to me that it is significant. A person's pride and arrogance can be the precipitating spiritual sickness that immobilizes them. Pride goes before a fall (Proverbs 16:18). The most dramatic example is Satan, himself as he is now forever consigned to being stuck in hell and subsequently the lake of fire for eternity. This cause should be self-evident to every believer.

I was recently watching an Australian-based television show revolving around a competition to decide who runs the best bed and breakfast establishment. The couples were mostly ordinary, average people who were appropriately humble about their homes and complimentary to others about their homes—except one couple. It was evident upon watching the first episode that this couple was arrogant, prideful, and self-consumed. As the season unfolded, their arrogance was almost too much to stomach as they disrespected their opponents and elevated their own skills and talents. The vindicating moment was at the conclusion of the series when it came time to choose between a humble mother-and-son team and this arrogant twosome. The mother and son came forth as victors and their beautiful bed and breakfast is now number one in all of Australia. It was the quintessential picture of how a person's pride is their own undoing.

We Commit Willful Sin.

The way of those who choose to break God's laws and precepts will inevitably be hard (Proverbs 13:15). Sin always has wages (Romans 6:23). Sometimes the repercussion of willful disobedience is getting stuck.

I am well aware that many people seem to go forward despite their lack of concern with regard to holiness and righteousness. I understand that the wicked can and do prosper and experience promotion. I have no easy answers except to say that the brokenness of this world can be navigated quite expertly by those who are equally as broken. However, to those of us who claim the name of Jesus as our personal Savior, the rules of progress are different. Willful disobedience can put a stop to a number of things. It is vital in moments of situational paralysis that a person take spiritual inventory and make sure they have clean hands and hearts before the Lord.

We Live In Fear.

Most people have heard of the story of Job, a righteous man who was in covenant with God yet found himself in the most challenging of all scenarios. He lost his family and his fortune and found himself seemingly stuck in this adversity with no discernible way out. Most people don't like the issues presented in the book of Job because it begins to untangle the mystery of God and how He may allow things to happen in our life. The good news of the book is, of course, Job's restoration once he prayed for his friends (Job 42:10). One of the keys, however, as to why this moment may have presented itself to Job is found through Job's own confession when he said,

> The thing I greatly feared has come upon me, and what I dreaded has happened to me. (Job 3:25)

How much of our lives is ruled by fear? How many decisions are made in our lives with fear being the driving force behind those decisions? Fear paralyzed the children of Israel from going into the Promised Land and caused them to be stuck in the wilderness for forty years. Fear paralyzed the rich young ruler from following Jesus and caused him to be stuck in the place of guilt and greed. The servant who buried his small talent in the ground, in the parable of the talents that Jesus told his disciples, feared losing what little he had gained. How many career choices are based upon fear of outcomes? How many relationships stay and go based on fear? How much destiny is forfeited because fear immobilizes the person from saying yes to God? Many people do not understand that fear and faith work very similarly in a person's life. While faith is required for any step forward, fear is what manifests when a person becomes stuck and entrenched. Consider the contrast:

Faith is confidence in what God has said.
Fear is confidence in what the situation or adversary is saying.

Faith connects you to the promises of God.
Fear connects you to the probabilities of the moment.

Faith is your "title" to something good from God.
Fear is your "title" to what you speculate in the natural.

Faith is your step into the future God has prepared for you.
Fear is your step into the ditch to which the enemy wants
to detour you.

We all face fears on occasion. However, the establishing and perpetuating of fears of any kind can be a cause for immobilization.

We Practice Unbelief, Doubt, And Procrastination.

Closely related to fear is the trinity of paralysis: unbelief, doubt, and procrastination. All of these are closely related and produce immobilization. A case could be made that these three are cousins to fear, but I felt they needed their own emphasis to underscore the point that how we view and approach the future is directly related to our ability to move forward. It takes no great revelation to understand that your inability to believe and act on that belief will keep you in the place you currently find yourself in. I certainly would never endorse a bad decision, but inevitably a circumstance will arise in which a decision has to be made and putting it off simply will not work.

Sometimes life presents what I call "log jams," in which circumstances are so twisted that there is no apparent, obvious, or easy decision to be made and God's direction at the moment can feel elusive. Many people's tendency is to procrastinate because of their doubt of direction at the moment. Listen carefully—there is an appropriate and needed truth concerning waiting on God. These moments will take incredible spiritual discernment. That being said, some situations have a due date where a decision must be made. It is at that point procrastination must be challenged. Be wise and understand that these things can cause a self-inflicted "stuck" situation.

We Are Bound By Tradition
(Mindsets, Mentalities, And Assumptions).

Mark Twain said that the only person who really enjoys change is a wet baby. My wife might disagree with that as she loves adventure and change, but I ascribe that basically to those with sanguine personalities. However, Twain had a point that in general most people have a difficult time moving beyond the boundaries of tradition, preference, and assumption. When these people become entrenched and immobilized, they tend to decorate it and simply live in it.

One cannot help but think of the religious leaders (Pharisees and

Sadducees) of Jesus' time. These people were "committed" to God but immobilized in an obsolete system of worship that was blinding them from seeing the truth of the Messiah (Savior and Deliverer) and paralyzing them from moving forward into "the acceptable year of the Lord" (Luke 4:19). Many people want to move forward, but only if they can maintain the same mind-sets, mentalities, and traditions that got them stuck in the first place.

Perhaps as we end this chapter this would be a good moment for you, the reader, to do some spiritual inventory and ask yourself about lingering causes and emotions immobilizing you from moving forward. As was mentioned, this list is by no means exhaustive but merely an opportunity to prime the pump of your discernment to evaluate any causes immobilizing you. Ask the Lord to reveal things that may have been overlooked or cleverly disguised by other ways of defining them (for example, calling bitterness "brute honesty" or criticalness "godly discernment"). Redefining a toxic emotion or mentality will do you no favors in moving forward. Your future and purposes are too important for you to continue carrying the regret of a self-inflicted "stuck."

Chapter Six

❖ ❖ ❖

Ancillary Problems Of Being Stuck

There may be no greater example of being stuck than the hundreds of years of slavery of Israel from after the time of Joseph to the revealing of Moses, their deliverer. These years of slavery are not chronicled in the Bible in detail, but to understand what this immobilizing circumstance must have been like is not hard to surmise. Generation after generation of slavery slowly and perhaps quite imperceptibly began to change mentalities, perspectives, and worldview. What started out in the beginning as an obvious injustice easily morphed into normal existence. What was initially unacceptable eventually became acceptable and normal.

The monotony of slave labor and toil simply became the routine of every waking moment of every day and there was no reason to assume it could ever change. Perhaps not every Israelite thought this way, but enough of them did to ostensibly immobilize the whole nation, which consisted of millions of people. When Moses entered the scene, his ministry of deliverance was one to change not only the mind of a Pharaoh but also literally a nation of slaves. I am always struck by the account in Exodus revealing their mentalities after being released through the manifestation of many signs and wonders and then coming up to the Red Sea with Pharaoh's army hot on their heels—their mentality was one of wanting to go back to their "stuck" situation.

> And when Pharaoh drew near, the children of Israel lifted their eyes, and behold, the Egyptians marched after them. So they were very afraid, and the children of Israel cried out to the Lord. Then they said to Moses, "Because there were no graves in Egypt, have you taken us away to die in the wilderness? Why have you so dealt with us, to bring us up out of Egypt? Is this not the word that we told you in Egypt, saying, 'Let us alone that we may serve the Egyptians'? For it would have been better for us to serve the Egyptians than that we should die in the wilderness." (Exodus 14:10–12)

The most dangerous susceptibility you may face in your "stuck" season is to allow your disposition and attitude to consider this situation normal. That is what the enemy will try to do. He will endeavor to get into your mind and worldview to convince you that what you are currently facing is what you will always endure. This is the reason people stay stuck in long-term abusive relationships, dead-end jobs, and addictive patterns. Their immobilization has existed for such a long time that it has become their normal.

> ❖ ❖ ❖
>
> **The most dangerous susceptibility you may face in your "stuck" season is to allow your disposition and attitude to consider this situation normal.**

I have counseled some people who have grown up in incredibly dysfunctional homes and atmospheres. From their earliest memory their homes were full of deviance, mental abuse, and codependent enablement. When they are released from that environment into early adulthood and seek relationship with people from a genuinely normal childhood, chaos erupts as to what the real definition of "normal" is to be. The years of dysfunctional environment have conditioned them to believe that their "stuck" is normal. I liken it to several useful illustrations.

When Tracie and I were first married we lived in an affordable town house located next to a train track. The reason the townhouse was so affordable was due to the fact that when trains sped by at least four times a day, it felt as if the whole building were shaking and the noise was incredible. I can still remember vividly those first weeks of living in this town house that when the train sped through there was no ignoring it. If it went through in the middle of the night it would wake you up by its thundering roar. It was an embarrassment to have guests over for dinner or a simple visit.

I knew that this housing arrangement was temporary, but I thought there was no way a person could ever get used to it. Strangely enough, after a few short months the train roar and vibration were hardly noticeable. I ceased being awakened at night and it didn't really seem to bother me much. In fact, the only time I might have noticed it was when I was on the kitchen phone talking to someone. If the train roared by at the same moment I was on the phone, the person on the other end would often say, "What is that sound?" My reply would be, "Sorry—that's the train in the backyard. I don't notice it anymore." My circumstances had become my normal.

In Charleston, South Carolina, there is a large paper mill on the northwest side of town. If the wind blows the right direction the odor of the plant can be smelled from just about anywhere in a three-county region. The odor is not pleasant. It is a cross between a recently used locker room, the stagnant smell of marshlands, and a recently used bathroom. It is bad.

When we first moved to the area and the kids were little, we would often drive by the plant on the interstate getting to needed appointments. When the smell hit us, it would suddenly get silent in the car. We would start looking at each other with accusing glances. The older boys, who knew where the smell originated, would often look at their younger sister and ask, "Kalyn, was that you?" Her indignation was swift and loud:

"No, it was not!" The car would roar in laughter. However, after we had lived in the area for twenty-two years, the odor, which was sharply pungent to the most damaged sense of smell, had suddenly seemed to fade away.

The question is "Why?" Had the paper mill devised an odorless method of manufacturing paper products? Hardly. What changed was our sense of the normality of the odor. Our noses simply got used to it. It was our normal. The only time our sense of smell might be awakened was if a guest was in town and they would make mention of it. If you lived in Charleston, that smell was a part of package deal.

This is the dangerous susceptibility of a "stuck" season or circumstance. You start to see it as your forever "normal." How many people have learned to live with the stench in their lives, their relationships, their careers, and their spiritual lives and simply accept it as normal?

My youngest son was a college football player and had three roommates who were athletes too. Whenever we would visit him at school and open the door to his room, the stench would nearly knock us over. Their room smelled like a musty locker room. My wife would say, "Tyler, can't you all smell that?" His answer was a consistent "What smell?" The stench was their normal. The children of Israel had lived in the stench and "stuck" place of slavery for so long that it had become their normal. The question now becomes, *is the place you find yourself stuck your new normal?*

Have you accepted as normal that a promotion just isn't in the works for you? Have you accepted as normal that you aren't bright enough to go back to school? Are you living in an abusive or toxic relationship and have simply resigned yourself that it is your normal? Do you think normal is facing the bondages and addictions that hold your life? These types of thoughts are the susceptibilities of living in immobilized circumstances.

The other susceptibility in a "stuck" circumstance is to open a "door" in your mind or your spirit to demonic activity and reaction. An "open door" is a metaphor that is used at times to indicate an event or trauma that has impacted you to such a degree that the enemy (devil) is able to exploit that event by provoking other emotions and reactions in your life. It's literally as if the devil can walk into your life through this open door and wreak havoc. Open doors are the devil's playground.

It's not enough to simply deal with the repercussions of the trauma, but now a host of other emotions can find their way into your life. Whenever a sense of forward movement is gone and the potential causes mentioned in the previous chapter are left unaddressed, an open door can occur through the frustration or fear that may be present. From this there can arise reactions that are negative, unproductive, and even dangerous.

> **Open doors are the devil's playground.**

I mentioned in a previous chapter the poor decision I made to move to a church in Oakland, California. It was a situation that had become stuck due to a self-inflected desire to do my own agenda without consulting or asking the Lord. There were a number of causes present that exploited my bad decision. It was a crucible of pain whose lessons are forever etched on my mind. The stress of the ministry that took place there not only affected my own mental and emotional health but was taking its toll on my wife and our relationship.

After just a few weeks of living and ministering in the San Francisco area, it became clear that I had missed the will of God and put myself in an untenable situation. I will be the first to teach that God may and will often "call" you into tough assignments. Pain and difficulty are not necessarily the signs of a bad decision. That being said, when there is no grace or anointing for the task, a person must of necessity reevaluate their mission and, in this case I had completely done my will rather than His. The pain and darkness became so great that a myriad of emotions began flooding over me because of the open doors I had allowed through my ignorance of such things. I literally fell into what I now believe was a clinical depression.

Out of the frustration of the situation a great deception sought to blanket me. There were moments of anger, fear, panic, revenge, and blame-shifting. My poor wife endured a husband who I am sure at times looked as though he was losing it. I would come home after the day's work and climb up to the third floor of the parsonage and sit in a rocker in a dark room and simply rock back and forth in silence. These were not the actions of a normal person. These were the actions of a man being exploited by the enemy through an open door.

I eventually went to a psychologist in a desperate effort to shake free from the overwhelming sense of discouragement. It was of little value as the frustration, fear, and panic only increased and entrenched themselves. Breaking this stronghold and closing the door would eventually take an intervention of the Lord both spiritually and through some providential orchestration of His hand. I found people who understood what was going on and could agree with me in authority to close those doors and move forward.

The point I am endeavoring to make is that a "stuck" season is an opportune moment for the devil to treat your mind and life as a playground for his torment. This is what happened to the children of Israel in the previous passage. Despite their personal and corporate experiences of seeing God's hand move for them in the past, they did not recognize that they had opened a door to a deception that produced their frustration, panic, fear, anger, and blame-shifting. It was so profound that they now blamed Moses, who had been used of God to supernaturally deliver them, for bringing them to the moment of destruction—rather than accepting responsibility and trusting God at their moment of need.

I would never suggest that I am in the league of Moses when it comes to ministry, but I can identify with the dynamics of the situation in Exodus 14. As a pastor, your desire is to help people break free from their paralysis and immobilization in life. Often that entails counseling, teaching, and even supernatural impartation of anointing. The greatest joy of a genuine pastor is to see people delivered, set free, and move forward. However, it is not uncommon as the next crisis moment appears in people's lives that their frustration and anger shift to the very person who previously helped deliver them. This is because of the realities of open doors. If one does not deal with and release the root cause of the immobilization, it will simply come back, and you will repeat the pattern of the past.

For me, as embarrassed as I am to admit, the "causes" of my poor decision to move were based on offense, pride, and carnal ambition. Those open doors became the devil's playground to lead me into a deep depression. The susceptibility became reality because I did not recognize the dynamics of my circumstances. Had I not released these things, I might still be stuck.

There is a story concerning trappers in Africa who target monkeys as their prey. They leave the front gate of the cage open with a piece of meat enticing the monkeys to enter, thereby trapping them and causing them to be stuck in the cage; but the monkeys are too smart to simply walk in the front. Instead, the monkeys reach in from the side of the cage and grab the meat through the bars. The trappers are smarter and make the meat too large to slip through the bars. When a monkey tries to pull the meat out, it can't. It will screech and scream, but it will not let it go, thereby immobilizing itself anyway. The trapper then simply walks up, knocks it on the head, and has himself a monkey. The moral of the story is "Let it go, monkey!"

This is a silly story but applicable with regard to those who find themselves stuck and refusing to understand their susceptibilities. Before you are in a position to move forward, you must be sure you are not seeing your circumstance as normal and refusing to close those open doors by letting your issues go.

In just a moment we are going to turn the corner from analyzing our paralysis and immobilization to implementing some principles, precepts, and wisdom to get our lives moving forward again. I have used Exodus 14:10–12, to illustrate the susceptibilities of the Israelites' mentality. Before we leave the account, it is fascinating to share here, by way of preparation for what is ahead, the words Moses received from the Lord with which he exhorted the Israelites.

> And Moses said to the people, "Do not be afraid. Stand still, and see the salvation of the Lord, which He will accomplish for you today. For the Egyptians whom you see today, you shall see again no more forever. The Lord will fight for you, and you shall hold your peace." And the Lord said to Moses, "Why do you cry to Me? Tell the children of Israel to go forward. But lift up your rod, and stretch out your hand over the sea and divide it. And the children of Israel shall go on dry ground through the midst of the sea. (Exodus 14:13–16)

If I might briefly synopsize Moses' remarks to the immobilized, he said,

> Let go of fear.
> Be at rest.
> Get a vision for your future.
> God's got this.
> Quit your whining.
> It's time to move forward.

As you turn the page to a new chapter in this book, let us turn the page to a new chapter in *your life.*

PART II — THE PATH TO BECOMING UNSTUCK

Chapter Seven

❖ ❖ ❖

Perspective, Not Panic

Both of my parents were from a very small town in a rural part of north-central Kansas. Both of my grandfathers were farmers and it could be said without embellishment that nearly everyone in that small town, whether directly or indirectly, was connected and had a relationship at some level to agriculture. The whole economy of the region was tied to the success of the farmer, so farming was important and serious business. It should come as no surprise having this kind of family roots that a part of my work résumé would include time spent on the farm.

From the moment my foot was able to depress a clutch on a tractor at age thirteen to my senior year in high school, I spent summers working on the farm with one of my uncles. I have so many fond memories of that period because it taught me so many important life lessons. One of the most memorable lessons revolved around getting stuck.

The lesson begins by understanding the culture of the farm with regard to work ethic and individual responsibility. The farm is a constant swirl of important activities that cannot be neglected or overlooked. There were always chores to be done, cattle to be fed, and fields needing to be worked. There were tractors, trucks, combines, and various implements to help work the land. If you were a large farm owner, you would naturally disperse all the responsibilities to the various farmhands who worked for you. Through delegation more work could be accomplished in a day. Often these responsibilities would fall to family members, both male and female, at as early an age as possible. That meant, right or wrong, a young teenager often found himself driving trucks and tractors valued at tens if not hundreds of thousands of dollars.

To say the least, it was an incredibly awesome experience as a thirteen-year-old boy to find myself on top of a gigantic piece of equipment controlling the wheel as I made my way through a field. This act would thrust an immature teen-aged boy front and center into responsibility. As I reflect, my uncle was always careful to measure responsibility and mentor his farmhands appropriately before simply throwing us the keys to a tractor; however, there was no doubt a young man grew up quickly working on the farm. As with most teenagers I suppose, I always felt my maturity and skill levels were beyond my uncle's comfort levels for responsibility. My attitude was always "Throw me the keys—I'm ready to roll." It never seemed like work, but it actually had a built-in fun factor due to the machinery. I loved it—until that day I got stuck.

The normal protocol of plowing a field was to have my uncle take me to the field and I would climb into the tractor cab with him as he would "open" the field. Opening a field was simply making a couple of initial laps around the grounds with my uncle pointing out to me certain areas of the field that might be problematic or need to be avoided. Perhaps the field had a dangerous slope in one area that could potentially tip the tractor over, or maybe there had been an old stone foundation in an area years ago that was now hidden by a few inches of dirt and could break the tips of the plow. His knowledge and expertise in these matters could actually be lifesaving information.

This day, because of his farm schedule, I was being assigned a field to open by myself. It had been an exceptionally rainy spring and the ground was moist and my uncle reminded me to watch carefully for exceptionally soggy areas that could cause even the most powerful and expensive tractor to get stuck. My teenaged head bobbed up and down acknowledging the instructions, but honestly I was more enamored and interested in mounting the giant tractor, starting the loud diesel engine, and tossing some dirt around. I drove to the field and started the lap to open up the field. Shortly into the lap I noticed an extremely dark place in the soil that obviously indicated there was wet ground ahead. There was no standing water, just darker soil, so I figured the ground to be moist, but certainly no impediment to the power of a mighty John Deere tractor. I plowed right through (no pun intended). You are undoubtedly guessing the end to this story.

Yep.

Stuck.

Very stuck.

Immobilized.

Going nowhere.

What's the first reaction a person exhibits once it's obvious he is stuck in a situation?

You may have guessed this too.

Panic.

I did everything I knew to somehow swiftly find a way to get "unstuck." I downshifted the tractor to its lowest gear. I rocked the tractor backward and forward by slipping the gears into reverse and first gears over and over. I spun the tires as if I were at the national tractor pull contest. My mind was racing trying to recover every word of instruction and experience my uncle may have shared with me, but initially it was all to no avail. In fact, the more I tried the more the panic began to set in, and with that panic the deeper my stuck tractor seemed to be getting.

Suddenly what seemed to be an easy assignment and one I was well prepared for became quite complicated and over my head. The wheels of the tractor were sinking more deeply into the ground with every rotation of their spinning. The tires looked to be at least halfway underground. I wanted to run somewhere and hide. How much trouble would I be in? I was dreading the possibilities of having to face my uncle. A hundred emotions were swirling through my body at this moment of being stuck. Everything from embarrassment to self-pity to anger was beginning to take root at that moment of realization I was stuck. All of it was being exploited by the pressure of panic.

When you are panicked you make quick, sometimes rash decisions. You may risk doing something that is beyond reason for the moment. Most of all, you probably try to hide and hope no one sees you and what is going on. In this instance I was able to patiently wait an hour or so and as the sun dried the ground around the wheels of the tractor, I was eventually able to pull myself out. The relief was palpable. However, I learned that panic was not my friend.

I tell this story as a springboard to the discussion of how we begin to get our lives unstuck and moving forward. You may have never been on a farm and couldn't care less about agricultural technique, but you can probably relate to the feelings of immobilization coupled with panic. Before I simply lay out some precepts and wisdom for your situation, let's catch our breath and instead of panicking, let's get some perspective.

Mark Twain said, "I am an old man and have known a great many troubles, but most of them have never happened." When we hit a difficulty that immobilizes us, our temptation is to panic. We begin to tell ourselves, "This is the worst thing that has ever happened to anyone. Nobody has ever faced this problem before."

The truth is that neither of those sentences is true, and as real and as powerful as your current difficulty may be, most difficulties are not as bad as they initially appear. It's the panic that exasperates the immobilization. A *Newsweek* magazine article, published in the mid-1990s, titled "Exhausted" explored the cultural need to solve problems instantly. The writer stated,

A frazzled America, stressed as never before. Why? Because we have cell phones in cars and beepers on belts and we carry them to Disney World, the beach, and the bathroom. We think the world will fall apart if we can't respond right now. Life, everything in life, becomes an emergency.

This is exactly the dynamic when it comes to getting stuck. We panic and expend untold amounts of emotional energy attempting to spin our way out rather than taking a moment to gain some perspective.

I was a staff pastor for almost ten years at a notable church in the upstate of South Carolina in the late 1980s and early 1990s. Prior to becoming a staff pastor, I had been a lead pastor for several years. I always knew the day would arrive when a door would open for me to give pastoral leadership to a congregation again, but at this particular time, especially after a difficult departure from a denomination, this staff position seemed best suited for me. The lead pastor of this notable church was a kind man who honestly did not have a place for me on his staff initially but saw the potential and calling in my life and made a place for me in the area of education.

My first assignment was to help start a Bible college, and during the years I was employed the college experienced remarkable success. It started with a class of seven students and the eventual enrollment eclipsed several hundred after a few years. A part of my responsibilities was not only the administration of the college but also the creation of curriculum that the school would use. I created over thirty college course curriculums during that time period.

Slowly, more and more responsibility was released to me that encompassed a number of areas of ministry. I was assigned to assimilate new members into the life of the church. I was assigned the Preparation for Ministry class, which prepared new members to serve in various areas of the life of the church. I was released to preach in the pulpit when the senior pastor was away with his many responsibilities. I assisted the pastor in supporting numerous local churches that looked to our church for help and wisdom. My wife and I started a young adult program called "Master's Commission." We spent time every day each week inputting into their lives at various levels and training them for future ministry.

However, in the midst of all this profitable and important ministry,

I was plagued by these feelings of being stuck. I knew my call was to eventually lead a church as the point pastor, but at this moment despite the incredible opportunity I was given and the impactful ministry that was taking place, I struggled with these feelings of being stuck. Instead of having perspective concerning the time and place I was in, I allowed panic to push me internally.

It is interesting to analyze how panic manifests in a person's life. For me, I started to live in what I now define as "life increments." I started to say to myself (and to God), "Surely by the end of the year some door will open up for me." When the end of the year arrived, I would then say, "Surely by the spring something will change." Once spring arrived it would be, "Surely by the time school starts again in the fall our situation will change and a church or opportunity will present itself." I lived this way for nearly eight years, undoubtedly driving my wife crazy. I could never get perspective concerning the season I was in but rather was living life in these artificial four-to-six-month increments that I had created because of this panic I had allowed to exist. This panic convinced me that my prime years were escaping me and I needed to get unstuck from where I was and move on to where I thought I needed to be. I missed so many important moments those years, especially with my boys and their activities, as I focused on the next door of opportunity rather than maximizing the season in which I was living.

It is critically important before I outline some ideas about springing out of your paralysis and immobilization that you take a moment to get the proper perspective of your current situation. If you are feeling stuck even though you are in a divinely ordained season, then this perspective will help keep your panic from making decisions that may not be optimum for what God is forging in your life.

As I typed the list above concerning all the important and powerful ministry opportunities I was given at that local church, I can now, years later, clearly see how God was training me and enlarging me for some things He would want me to do in the future. However, throughout those years I had allowed panic to cloud my perspective. Victor Frankl, the

Viennese psychoanalyst and Holocaust survivor noted earlier, stated, "When we are no longer able to change a situation, we are challenged to change ourselves." This is where we must start in our quest for moving forward. What needs to be changed in us and not only our situation?

However, if your paralysis and immobilization is due to poor decision-making or an attack from the enemy, then you must begin to arise and pursue your future in a far more aggressive way.

A story in 2 Kings 7 introduces four lepers who were in just such a situation that eclipsed their ability to change it. The King of Syria had moved against Israel and strategically exploited an opportune moment in a time of famine. The Scripture tells us that the famine was so desperate and expansive that the people had literally turned to cannibalism (2 Kings 6:28-29). If such a scene was the plight of "normal" Israelites, what might four lepers be made to endure seeing that not only their country was under siege from the enemy and food was nearly impossible to find, but their personal conditions prohibited them from much, if not all, interaction with others? It was beyond bad; it was desperate and seemingly impossible to correct.

> ❖ ❖ ❖
>
> "What do we have to lose?" There comes a moment in your immobilization when your desperation brings you to that question.

A conversation arises from these four lepers with regards to their plight and their options. The conversation-starter was in the form of a question among the four:

"Why are we sitting here until we die?" (2 Kings 7:3)

To put this question in modern colloquial terms, they were simply saying, "What do we have to lose?" There comes a moment in your immobilization when your desperation brings you to that question. It's almost as if it's a point of embarrassment. We know it should be different, but it's as if a light turns on and you receive an epiphany that whatever it was that was holding you back is no longer your greatest concern. These lepers looked at their situation and understood that their choice to go forward in this desperate situation was actually quite simple.

> "If we say, 'We will enter the city,' the famine is in the city, and we shall die there. And if we sit here, we die also. Now therefore, come, let us surrender to the army of the Syrians. If they keep us alive, we shall live; and if they kill us, we shall only die." (2 Kings 7:4)

❖ ❖ ❖

A. W. Tozer once wrote, "If you feel that where you are is where you ought to be, you will remain right where you are."

What did they have to lose? Absolutely nothing. For them it wasn't panic as much as priority. If they were going to die, then they might as well go out swinging. They understood the perspective of where they found themselves and this was the moment to make a decision. A. W. Tozer once wrote, "If you feel that where you are is where you ought to be, you will remain right where you are." In the lepers' case, that no longer made any sense. Whatever fears they may have harbored were now eclipsed by the corner they found themselves in. They were ready to move forward.

What about you? Is it time to move forward? Are you simply in a panic and perhaps need to evaluate who the author of your "stuck" situation may be, or do you have the perspective you need? If you are in a God-ordained sovereign moment, then my counsel would be to embrace these moments and let the Lord forge you in character and bring forth the purposes He has planned. If you are convinced you are where you are because of poor decisions or even the enemy himself, then read carefully these next chapters as I offer you a path out.

Chapter Eight

❖ ❖ ❖

Steps Out Of Your "Stuck"

Soren Kierkegaard, the Danish philosopher and cultural critic, would often take aim at religious and societal ills by mocking it through the use of parable. He would attend all the social elite's parties and gatherings and would laugh with them and appear as one of them, all the while gathering insight and information about their worldview, which he would later anonymously mock. His critiques through these stories were often times searing. One of his notable stories was titled "The Wild Duck of Denmark." The parable went as follows:

A wild duck was flying northward with his mates across Europe during the springtime. In route, he happened to land in a barnyard in Denmark, where he quickly made friends with the tame ducks that lived there. The wild duck enjoyed the corn and fresh water. He decided to stay for an hour, then for a day, then for a week, and finally, for a month. At the end of that time, he contemplated flying to join his friends in the vast North land, but he had begun to enjoy the safety of the barnyard, and the tame ducks had made him feel so welcome. So, he stayed for the summer.

One autumn day, when his wild mates were flying south, he heard their quacking. It stirred him with delight, and he enthusiastically flapped his wings and rose into the air to join them. Much to his dismay, he found that he could rise no higher than the eaves of the barn. As he waddled back to the safety of the barnyard, he muttered to himself, "I'm satisfied here, I have plenty of food, and the area is good. Why should I leave?" So, he spent the next winter on the farm.

In the spring, when the wild ducks flew overhead again, he felt a strange stirring in his breast, but he did not even try to fly up to meet them. When they returned in the fall, they again invited him to rejoin them, but this time, the duck did not even notice them. There was no stirring within his breast. He simply kept on eating the corn which made him fat.

Kierkegaard's parable is clear. The duck is stuck because he refused to take the steps to get out of his self-imposed circumstances. There were moments that the internal feeling to fly forward was there, but the comfort of the barnyard was too much to overcome, until finally the feeling to move forward faded away. Getting stuck does not always mean that the situation you are in is bad or traumatic. Sometimes it is simply too comfortable and convenient a place, which slowly traps you into staying.

Years ago my wife and I made the decision that the doctrine we believed and the church structure that seemed most biblical could not fit and would not be embraced in the denomination we were connected to. We felt "led" to participate in what would eventually become known as the "non-denominational" world. We had no connections to it. There was no network of pastors or bishops to call and ask for help. We tried to figure out a way to easily move from one world to the next, but nothing seemed to be working. We had to simply trust God and take those steps necessary to reach the place we felt we needed to be and get out of the "stuck" we were currently enduring. Gratefully, God honored those steps and some amazing miracles and providences marked those incredible weeks and months.

After settling into our new assignment and experiencing some amazing moments of blessing and favor directly related to the faith steps we took, my phone began to ring from pastors of the denomination I had recently left. They too were feeling the pain of being stuck in some form of spiritual paralysis or organizational immobilization and were looking for help moving forward, perhaps even doing what I had done. I shared with them some wisdom I had gleaned from our faith steps, but interestingly, on several occasions the response would be something like "Kevin, I can appreciate what you are saying, but I need a smooth transition to get to where you are now. I can't take those sorts of risks." I didn't laugh; however, I did find it ironic how everyone wants the fruit of moving forward but few will embrace the steps and process of what it takes to get there. I understand the feeling completely. Kierkegaard's duck story illustrates it powerfully. Religion preaches a great theoretical journey, but there comes a moment when the person must actually take the step.

> Religion preaches a great theoretical journey, but there comes a moment when the person must actually take the step.

I am going to offer some general steps in what it normally entails to move forward out of your current situation and begin to walk toward your preferable future. I will stipulate that every person's situation will be unique and individualized. What my path may have been will undoubtedly look somewhat different than another's journey. That being said, the human condition at these moments has remarkable similarities as well. God is no respecter of persons (Romans 2:11). How He works with one He tends to work with all. So as you begin to read and meditate on what will follow, I encourage you to do so, not with a goal to apply these points with wooden or sterile acquiescence but rather an ear for the voice of the Holy Spirit in applying those points of obedience that fit in the path you may currently be walking.

Let's begin by analyzing a man who was incredibly stuck whom Jesus helped to get moving forward:

> After this there was a feast of the Jews, and Jesus went up to Jerusalem. Now there is in Jerusalem by the Sheep Gate a pool, which is called in Hebrew, Bethesda, having five porches. In these lay a great multitude of sick people, blind, lame, paralyzed, waiting for the moving of the water. For an angel went down at a certain time into the pool and stirred up the water; then whoever stepped in first, after the stirring of the water, was made well of whatever disease he had. Now a certain man was there who had an infirmity thirty-eight years. When Jesus saw him lying there, and knew that he already had been in that condition a long time, He said to him, "Do you want to be made well?" The sick man answered Him, "Sir, I have no man to put me into the pool when the water is stirred up; but while I am coming, another steps down before me." Jesus said to him, "Rise, take up your bed and walk." And immediately the man was made well, took up his bed, and walked. And that day was the Sabbath. (John 5:1–9)

Here is a man who has been stuck in his condition for thirty-eight years. Apparently he had been hanging around a lot of other people who not only *felt* stuck but were *legitimately* stuck as well.

The old secular proverb rings true at this point: "Birds of a feather flock together." Jesus saw the man and could discern that he had been immobilized for quite a long time. Perhaps it was a word of knowledge, for Jesus would have no problem supernaturally discerning such things. Or perhaps as we previously mentioned, a "stuck" person simply gives off a vibe that is easily identified. Perhaps it was frustration, bitterness, anger, self-pity, or any of the other associated emotions. The fact remains that Jesus wanted to help this man. In fact, what ultimately caught my attention in this story was that in the midst of a number of people who were feeling stuck, this man was the only person at this moment who got "unstuck." Isn't that remarkable? Many people desire moving forward, but could there be some key actions from those who actually do it and those who don't? I want to suggest some of the following.

A Passion To Move Forward

Jesus asked the question of this man stuck in his infirmity for decades, "Do you want to be made well?" (*v.* 6). What kind of question is that? Of course he wanted to move forward. This man was at the pool that could provide healing. Wasn't it obvious that he was looking for some help? Didn't his very location demonstrate some level of desire? Apparently not in the mind of Jesus. I can assure you that Jesus wasn't asking the question because He couldn't discern the moment. Jesus was asking the question in order for the man to do some important introspection. Exactly what was his desire level? How committed to change was this man?

Many people claim to want change. They will cry and moan for the opportunity to move forward. They declare loudly their desire to move forward and apprehend the future that is in front of them. Many go through the motions, much like this man who tried moving to the waters when they were "stirred." They attend church, go to seminars and special ministry sessions, and even attend small-group meetings. They make all the motions, each one good and needed, but the question remains: "Do you really want to get unstuck?" Are you simply going through the motions? Do you really want life to be different or have you simply grown accustomed to the ebb and flow of encouragement and despair? There must be an inner passion that is associated with the need to go forward.

Passion is not simply sentimentality or affection. It is not as fleeting as excitement or hype. It is our English word for what the Bible calls *zeal.* One Hebrew scholar stated that the etymology of the word *zeal* is what we might even call "fanatical." The Greek translation gives the impression of one who has abandoned himself to a cause. Passion is what we might call "next-level desire." There are many things we might say we desire in life, but that desire is easily detoured. Passion is another level of desire; in fact, it is uncommon desire. It wants something and it wants it badly.

Passion is a compelling thing. Passion exists when the popularity of a moment passes. Passion remains when one is tired and ready to throw in the towel. Passion keeps burning when no one else sees it, gets it, or wants it. Passion is 365 days a year, 7 days a week, 24 hours a day. Passion, in many ways, is the catalyst that provides the fuel to get you moving again.

❖ ❖ ❖

Passion, in many ways, is the catalyst that provides the fuel to get you moving again.

My worst subject in school was without a doubt science. I was simply not good at any form of science. However, everyone knows that to graduate from high school a student must pass a science class. I remember almost nothing from my science classes except for one concept and it is the word *catalyst*. When you were doing an experiment and you might desire to see an outcome more quickly than what might be normally expected, you would throw in a chemical called a catalyst, which would help cause a reaction that reduced the time for the original chemicals to work together.

Passion is a spiritual catalyst. You may be doing all the right things and going through all the right motions, and doing those things may indeed offer an open door out of the immobilization. However, when passion is added to the equation it becomes a catalyst that the Lord uses to speed up the spiritual reaction time. Passion, most often, is birthed out of desperation. When you reach the point at which you are desperate for change, it is remarkable how quickly the catalyst of passion can manifest. Jesus was unveiling and exposing the level of desperation and passion the man had.

Disconnecting from Enabling or Toxic Relationships

The pool at Bethesda was a gathering place for people who were stuck in their sicknesses and health problems (*v.* 3). I find it fascinating how many hospitals, including certain government hospitals, are named after this familiar healing pool in the Bible. Even in the first century the name "Bethesda" was associated with a hospital-like atmosphere.

Now there are no recorded conversations among the people waiting at the pool, so at this point I must do some sanctified speculation concerning what the talk may have been. We know that the prevailing philosophy around the pool was that the first one in was the only one who would be healed. In other words, those who would be stuck in their situations would be the vast majority of folks, and those healed and moving forward would be the few "lucky" ones. Let's distill that type of thinking just a little deeper. The philosophy of the pool was to be sick and stuck; that was the normal existence. To be whole and moving forward would be the exception rather than the rule. Can you imagine the conversations that must have taken place as people waited for the stirring of the pool?

"Why are you here? We don't need more people here. The pool is already too crowded."

"My situation is far worse than your situation, so you should give up your space waiting."

"Nobody is as stuck as I am."

"It seems to me that we ought to be lining up to the pool with the worst cases up close and nearest the pool and the less serious sicknesses to the rear."

This pool was "stuck central." Can you imagine the stampede to the pool when the waters began to stir? It had to look something like the doors at Walmart on a Black Friday shopping event: pushing, shoving, yelling, tripping, because only one was getting the miracle. It pitted people competing against each another rather than encouraging each other.

Outside of the mad dash, people were left to commiserate with each other during the waiting times, which simply reestablished and reaffirmed inside of one another the normality of their "stuck" situations. It was the worst of environments when it came to moving forward. This may be why Jesus began this conversation with the man. Jesus needed to break the mentality of this circumstance being the norm as well as the voices that were perpetually maintaining it.

There comes a moment when in order to move forward you must evaluate the voices you are listening to and the people you are hanging around. You must start recognizing "stuck" thinking. Sometimes the voices and relationships around us are doing more to maintain our immobilization rather than set us free for our future.

There is a proper and needful place for all sorts of "support" groups addressing the challenges and situations of life. We do need people at times who can relate to what we are facing and come alongside us. That being said, we are not designed or created to entrench in the support cycle. This is exactly the reason Jesus told the man, once healed, to "rise, take up your bed and walk." Jesus circumvents the line and mayhem at the pool, as well as telling the man that it is time to find a different place to hang out. I am sure the man, after being there for thirty-eight years, had made lots of friendships. As difficult as this point may sound, there comes a moment when we realize that the environment and the people that were keeping us immobilized must be forsaken. To move forward will mean that some things and people may get left behind.

Quit Making Excuses

Upon being asked by Jesus if he wanted to be well, the man responded with two interesting excuses. First, he stated that he had no one to help him into the pool; then he stated that others always beat him to the pool (v. 7). He was deflecting the question actually. Jesus asked if he wanted to be well. The answer could have been, and probably should have been, a simple yes or no. Instead, the man offered excuses and shifted the blame. In other words, his predicament was not his fault.

He was where he was in life because others had not come through for him, others had dropped the ball, and that is why he was stuck. He was in this circumstance because his friends, his family, and his church had not been there for him the way they should have been. It was simply not his fault.

A center fielder on a high school baseball team was having an exceptionally bad day at practice in the outfield. The coach was getting madder and madder at the player until he said, "Get in here and I'll go out and show you how it's done." The coach went out to center field and took some practice balls. The first one took a bad bounce and hit him in the mouth. The second one was lost in the sun and he dropped it. Another one came off the end of the bat spinning, and he dropped the routine line drive. The coach came in even angrier, grabbed the player, and said, "You idiot! You have center field so messed up that even I can't do anything with it!"

These are the sounds of the blame-shifter and excuse-finder. My situation and how it's been handled are not my fault. I always get the bad break. People are always cutting in line ahead of me. People have failed me. Life hasn't been fair to me. People have always stolen opportunities from me. I take no responsibility for where I am or how things have shaken out. This is endemic in our era. Some research was done with regard to insurance accident forms and why people got into automobile accidents. Some of the excuses are classic as to people avoiding responsibility.

"An invisible car came out of nowhere, hit my car, and then vanished away."
"As I reached the intersection, a hedge sprang up and obscured my vision."
"I pulled away from the side of the road, glanced at my mother-in-law, and headed over the embankment."
"The pedestrian had no idea as to which direction to go, so I ran over him."

"The telephone pole was approaching fast and I attempted to swerve out of its way when it struck me on the front end."

"The guy was all over the road and I had to swerve a number of times before I hit him."

"The indirect cause of this accident was a little guy in a small car with a big mouth."

We are wired to make excuses and shift the blame. This needs to stop and we need to take responsibility that we are committed to moving forward and not finding excuses.

An Openness To Unorthodox Steps

George Bernard Shaw wrote, "The reasonable man adapts himself to the world. The unreasonable man persists in trying to adapt the world to himself. Therefore, all progress depends upon the unreasonable man." Jesus looked at the man at the pool, thirty-eight years in his infirmity and paralysis, and told him to "rise, take up your bed and walk" (*v.* 8). It doesn't get much more unreasonable than that. Yet despite the shortcomings of the man and the environment in which he was paralyzed, he was open to doing something unorthodox and seemingly unreasonable.

I can almost say without qualification that people who spring out of "stuck" circumstances and begin to move forward will undoubtedly face a moment of an unorthodox step. Springing out of "stuck" moments is rarely conventional. If it were, more people would take a step. I am not talking about theological heresy or some cult-like craziness but rather a step of faith, which to the reasonable, even rational person might appear unreasonable, but to God it is an act of liberating obedience.

I am continually amazed when reading scripture at how many times the Lord instructs His people to do something which to others appears unreasonable. Noah builds an Ark before people even understood the concept of rain. Abraham moves his family to a place that he has never heard of. Joseph stores away seven years of grain in anticipation of a famine no one could have expected. Moses confronts a Pharaoh with no army or earthly weapon, leads millions of people into a wilderness with no food or water, and brings those people to the edge of a sea with the world's greatest army on its heels. Joshua marches the people around a fortified city seven times to see it fall. David defeats a giant with a simple stone. Nehemiah rebuilds a wall in a miraculous fifty-two days. Peter walks on water. Paul sends aprons and handkerchiefs abroad to heal people's diseases. The list is almost endless, but the point is universal.

God will undoubtedly ask from you an unorthodox step to spring out of your seemingly "stuck" moment. What might that step be? Only you will know as you seek the face of God and listen to His voice and respond to His instructions. I suspect that whatever He may ask, you will find a precedent from the Scriptures that will give you the confidence to move forward in its implementation.

Courage To Take A Step

John Wayne, the famous Hollywood actor, remarked, "Courage is being scared to death but saddling up anyway." Wayne was neither a theologian nor a philosopher, but he got it right. There comes a moment when a person simply summons the courage and takes the step. Ralph Waldo Emmerson put it this way:

Whatever you do you need courage. Whatever course you decide upon, there is always someone to tell you you were wrong. There are always difficulties arising which tempt you to believe your critics are right. To map out a course of action and follow it to the end requires some of the same courage a soldier needs. Peace has its victories, but it takes brave men to win them.

One of the most encouraging stories in the Bible of a courageous person desperate to move forward is found in 1 Kings 17. The story is worth taking the time to read carefully.

> Then the word of the Lord came to him, saying, "Arise, go to Zarephath, which belongs to Sidon, and dwell there. See, I have commanded a widow there to provide for you." So he arose and went to Zarephath. And when he came to the gate of the city, indeed a widow was there gathering sticks. And he called to her and said, "Please bring me a little water in a cup, that I may drink." And as she was going to get it, he called to her and said, "Please bring me a morsel of bread in your hand." So she said, "As the Lord your God lives, I do not have bread, only a handful of flour in a bin, and a little oil in a jar; and see, I am gathering a couple of sticks that I may go in and prepare it for myself and my son, that we may eat it, and die." And Elijah said to her, "Do not fear; go and do as you have said, but make me a small cake from it first, and bring it to me; and afterward make some for yourself and your son. For thus says the Lord God of Israel: 'The bin of flour shall not be used up, nor shall the jar of oil run dry, until the day the Lord sends rain on the earth.'" So she went away and did according to the word of Elijah; and she and he and her household ate for many days. The bin of flour was not used up, nor did the jar of oil run dry, according to the word of the Lord which He spoke by Elijah. (1 Kings 17:8–16)

The widow woman represents many who are stuck today in seemingly impossible circumstances. She was in a situation with no apparent way out and at the end of her rope. It was at this point that God asked her through the prophet to do something unreasonable, even ridiculous, in order that He might do something miraculous for her to move forward. Jesus would mention this woman because obviously she represents a rare breed of person. She was the only one courageous enough to entertain the radical idea of an unorthodox step to break the deadlock of famine and lack.

How many of us are willing to do something that courageous? How many are willing to risk everything and let go of what is not working in order to embrace an unorthodox, faith step? Why *wouldn't* someone let go of what's not working? Unfortunately, many people elect the safety of their current circumstances rather than the adventure of trusting God. Some will stay in their rut of safety and conventionality their entire lives and never move forward. Perhaps this woman had been of a similar mentality, but the desperateness of the moment caused her mind to shift to new possibilities.

God had a plan for this woman to move forward. He has a plan for you too. He could not do His plan alongside her plan to die. Her plan was to make a cake and die. Her plan was so far removed from God's plan that they could not work in conjunction with each other. He will not synthesize your plan and His plan together. You must abandon your plans and embrace the plan of God if you want a future.

Some of you who are reading this line at this moment need to realize that God's plan is to get you unstuck and mobilized in His will. However, His plan is not remotely like yours. You can either protect your "flour" and "oil," or you can courageously in faith release it as He tells you. You cannot walk with fools and expect the blessings that come to the wise. You cannot launch out into the deep to bring in a great catch of fish while you choose to stand on the shore. Jesus said, "If you want to find life, then you will have to lose it." If you try to protect what you have, you will never receive what God has for you.

The woman did what God asked. She abandoned her plan and ran with God's. That was the game-changer in her life. So many times in my own life getting unstuck was a simple act of obedience. I have found that people who remain stuck are not there because God has not talked to them, but rather they simply refuse to obey what He has been saying. The Lord says over and over again in Scripture, "*If you will, then I will.*"

He never says, "I will if you will sometime down the road when it's convenient or comfortable and we can negotiate the details." God looks for obedience—and that takes courage.

I can remember as if it were yesterday the moment I packed all my earthly possessions, which weren't much, in a Ryder truck along with my wife and two young boys and moved across the country out of Oakland, California, to pursue God's new season in upstate South Carolina. We decided to believe God and just take the step and put it all on the line. I had $300 cash in my pocket and enough left on a credit card to get us a few nights in some motels as we started the trek across America. People thought we had lost our minds. I had no job, no income, and no ministry assignment, but the Lord said it was time to take the step. Were there some challenging days? Of course. However, there were miracles that became the testimonies of a lifetime, and more than that, we moved from that place of immobilization to a new season the Lord had designed for us. I don't know what your next step may be, but as you seek the Lord and hear His voice, don't let conventionality steal a miracle.

Chapter Nine

❖ ❖ ❖

The Place Of Risk

Faith, obedience, courage, and moving toward the future all entail risk. You will never get unstuck until you come to terms with risk. You can look at all the inspirational characters and their stories in the Bible and invariably, somewhere in their journey, they had to navigate risk. It shall be for you as well. To move from being stuck as an apartment renter you will have to risk signing the papers and buying a house. To get out of being stuck at a dead-end job you will have to risk sending out your résumé as well as giving your two-weeks notice. To move from being stuck financially you may need to consider the risk of investing. To get out of friendships in which you feel stuck, you may need to risk reaching out and initiating other friendships. Risk is unavoidable when it is time to move forward.

❖ ❖ ❖

You will never get unstuck until you come to terms with risk.

Why don't people want to risk, especially if they're pursuing a better future? Why would someone decide to stay in a paralyzing place? There may be several reasons. It has been said that people would rather deal with the problems they currently have than deal with the unknown potential problems they might face if they moved forward. That could

be true. A known challenge might be more comforting to some than an unknown one. However, for most people risk is avoided because of three reasons.

People Like Anchors And Loathe Anarchy

Moving forward by its very nature demands that one pull up any anchors and sail ahead. This is not as easy or as simple as many make it sound. Most people's lives in the 21st century are filled with a certain level of anarchy and chaos. Technology and economic dynamics are changing so rapidly that people's heads and schedules are swirling. They desire a sense of stability. This desire is not altogether unreasonable; however, stability is often times used as a synonym for reluctance to change. Moving forward, even from a difficult place of immobilization, can appear to be soliciting more anarchy and instability in one's life. It is not unusual for people to camp in an unproductive place because they feel safer anchored to that circumstance rather than anchored to the living God who is bringing them out.

People Like The Established And Not The Experiment

There is a reason that the vast majority of the population are employees rather than entrepreneurs. Predictability is a premium for most people. Think about how we design our children's lives with regard to success. We create routines and predictability so they can have the best chance at what we feel will be success. Risk is not in the equation when it comes to designing their life. That shadow, even with its acknowledged merit, transfers into our latter years. We become risk-adverse. We gravitate toward the established paths and outcomes. We want a tried-and-true template that has been tested and can simply be implemented with no risk. The walk of faith can feel like this experiment of which no one knows the outcome. Therefore, we opt for the safe and established rather than the unexpected.

People Connect With The Familiar And Not The Foreign

This was never more illustrated than on one occasion as a pastor when I felt that our church was stuck and needed something to shake our lethargy. I came into the office one day and started to think about how I could get us as a congregation moving forward again in our thinking. A crazy but simple idea hit me. I would change the seating configuration in the sanctuary to a new formation. Instead of four sections with five aisles, I would rearrange it into three sections and lose the center aisle, which would result in only four aisles. Nothing that radical, one would suppose.

Guess what.

When people entered the sanctuary the following Sunday you would have thought they were entering a brand-new church or location. Many looked lost and confused. Several were heard saying, "Where will I sit?" despite having the choice of hundreds of chairs. The place was absolutely foreign to all their natural senses and they didn't know what to make of it. It was actually comical watching them figure out their new seating location. Some actually tried to sit in ostensibly the same spot they sat previously under the former configuration.

The same dynamic occurred some time later when our church moved from one location to another, creating an extra five to seven minutes of drive time for a small number of our congregants. You would have thought we had moved the church to a new state rather than just down the road. These silly illustrations illuminate the fact that people connect with familiar settings and environment. Most refuse to risk losing what they know and see to potentially apprehend what they don't know and cannot see.

> **Most refuse to risk losing what they know and see to potentially apprehend what they don't know and cannot see.**

To move forward will involve elements of risk. A faith walk and obedience to God will always challenge our comfort boundaries. Yet you cannot read the Scriptures without being confronted over and over again with the stories of faith, along with its risks, of those who moved forward with God. The greatest miracles will always be attached to the greatest risks.

Recently my wife and I were sitting down with our financial counselor in order to get our retirement monies in proper investment portfolios. Let me be clear: we don't have a lot of money. If I revealed the amount of our investment funds, most people would laugh at how small an amount it truly is. The reason is that through the years we have emptied our savings accounts on at least three separate occasions for various kingdom projects at the direction of the Lord. We don't regret a single time because we know that big miracles demand big faith, and that involves risk. However, we were able to invest some monies towards our future and sought the advice of a qualified Christian financial planner.

> **The greatest miracles will always be attached to the greatest risks.**

As he was explaining our options, the principle of investment became ever so clear. If you desire greater yields, it will by necessity involve greater risks with your principal money. Lower yields have lower risks. This is not a great revelation for most people, but it is important to be reminded that your future promise may demand some risk on your part. What that risk may be only God knows for you. Mine has included things like leaving a stable denomination for the adventure of non-denominational life, starting a new church with no money, moving across the country, giving away my best automobile, emptying out my savings accounts, retiring from senior pastoring to a new expression of ministry, leaving a familiar city and friends for a new city to make new friends—and the list could on. I don't know how our family's risk experience stacks up to others, but I suspect we are close to expertise status.

I want to offer a quick list of principles we use to determine our risk tolerances and discern the leading of the Lord in these moments of feeling stuck.

Consider All Your Options

The simple believes every word, but the prudent considers well his steps. (Proverbs 14:15)

Considering your options includes evaluating what kind of "stuck" you are in as well as the possible solutions or moves you may need to make. Talk with trusted friends and advisors who have no agenda in your decision and who will help you sort out the moment with clarity. I have found that ambiguity is a bad place to make a good decision. The more clarity and possibilities you can envision or discern, the better you will feel when it comes time to obey God in the direction He will lead.

Sometimes when we are feeling stuck or paralyzed by our circumstances it is hard to dream and envision for the future. However, this is still an important place to keep that in mind, because if you are eventually going to take a step out of this moment, you need to make sure, inasmuch as it is within the will of God, that you step toward that promise however unconventional it may appear at the moment.

Consider The Cost

For which of you, intending to build a tower, does not sit down first and count the cost, whether he has enough to finish it. (Luke 14:28)

Every decision has a cost associated to it. It is immature to think that your decisions to move from the place you are currently stuck in will incur no cost. The cost may include financial considerations, but those are not the only costs. Perhaps moving forward may cost you some relationships, job security, or a comfortable location. Are you willing to absorb the cost of the step? Are you willing to embrace the responsibility for the decision and refuse to blame anyone for the outcome? Are you willing to endure sideline critics and well-meaning, rear-view-mirror counselors who don't understand what faith may look like?

To count the cost does not mean to avoid the cost. It means that once you embrace what that cost may be, you follow it through.

Pray For Guidance

If any of you lacks wisdom, let him ask of God, who gives to all liberally and without reproach, and it will be given to him. (James 1:5)

This should go without mentioning; however, it is amazing how little prayer is practiced in those moments of immobilization. Again, the only way you can identify the cause of your "stuck" situation is by seeking the Lord and understanding the moment. If God is accomplishing a work in your life through your current situation, then that revelation itself may keep you from making a poor decision by jumping from this place of instruction. If on the other hand you are in this circumstance due to something self-inflected, then the Lord can begin to guide, direct, and bring leadership to your next steps. Prayer in the early stages of analysis will be vital.

Visualize The Results

By faith he forsook Egypt, not fearing the wrath of the king; for he endured as seeing Him who is invisible. (Hebrews 11:27)

Visualization has taken its criticism from many who instantly associate it with "New Age" or Eastern religious practices. Let me be clear—any practice of visualization outside of a biblically grounded approach is off limits. The devil has made a practice of counterfeiting, convoluting, and twisting legitimate scriptural practice to make us fearful of doing something forbidden or dishonoring to God. The truth is, a faith walk is not a blind walk. We are not in the dark with regard to numerous things. In the passage above, Moses did not fear the one whom he could see with natural eyes because he had his spiritual eyes on God and the promise of deliverance. Abraham was escorted outside his tent and told to look at the stars in the night sky and to envision a nation. If you have a clear promise from God that is based on His Word, then to visualize your future is a part of your walk by faith.

Announce The Decision

(as it is written, "I have made you a father of many nations") in the presence of Him whom he believed—God, who gives life to the dead and calls those things which do not exist as though they did. (Romans 4:17)

I can remember clearly, after receiving an unmistakable call to preach the gospel and go into the ministry, that my announcement of such was met with more than a little skepticism from some. Where I was and who I had been did not line up with the announcement I was making. However, I quickly learned and understood that spiritual reality is activated through the words of our mouth. As we make our confession, a spiritual activation takes place. The best illustration is the actual activity of receiving salvation. Paul writes clearly in Romans 10:8–10,

But what does it say? "The word is near you, in your mouth and in your heart" (that is, the word of faith which we preach): that if you confess with your mouth the Lord Jesus and believe in your heart that God has raised Him from the dead, you will be saved. For with the heart one believes unto righteousness, and with the mouth confession is made unto salvation.

In other words, your part was right belief and the confession of that belief, which activated salvation. You didn't simply "think" yourself saved, but rather you spoke that which you were convinced of in your heart. In much the same way, we must announce and speak those things that the Lord has spoken and that we believe. The spoken announcement begins to activate the reality of those promises into our lives.

Let Go Of The Old

Brethren, I do not count myself to have apprehended; but one thing I do, forgetting those things which are behind and reaching forward to those things which are ahead. (Philippians 3:13)

You cannot drive forward by staring in the rearview mirror. There will be things, both endearing and offending, you will have to let go of. When I decided at the age of fifty-nine that it was God's will and timing to leave a thirty-five-year history of pastoring to step into the next season of my life and ministry, there were a number of things that I would need to let go of. I had so many wonderful church members that had to be let go of and released to new pastors in their lives. I had to let go of the dreams and hopes I had carried for that city. I had to let go of the security, visibility, and honor that was generated from being a full-time senior pastor. I had to let go of a city that had been my home for decades. These were just some of the things that had to be released to spring from the place where I was stuck.

Take The Step

We walk by faith, not by sight. (2 Corinthians 5:7)

Nike has a familiar slogan, "Just do it." There comes a moment when the analysis, evaluation, prayer, and counsel come to an end and you simply make the decision to take the step. No one can do that for you.

In the film *Indiana Jones and the Last Crusade* there is a scene toward the end of his adventure in search for the mythical Holy Grail when Indiana Jones must prevail over three tests, which are actually booby traps, in order to enter the room that holds the cup of Christ. Each of these tests is outlined in a book that his father has created through his research in order to assist the one on such a quest. The quest for the Grail is all the more vital as his father has been shot and needs a miracle, which only the Grail can produce.

One of those tests appears to be a step off a cliff that drops into a vast abyss. To the natural eye, such a step would result in assured death. Indiana, realizing that his father, who has been shot and is dying in the other room, knows that the only way to "cure" him is to have him drink from the chalice. Indiana has a decision to make. Will he believe his natural eyes, or will he trust the directions found in the book to take a leap of faith into a seemingly deep abyss? He decides to take the step and lands on a ledge that has been cleverly camouflaged from his sight at the edge of the abyss. His leap of faith ultimately is the springboard in saving his father's life.

So it is with you. Your step of faith may not be as dramatic, nor may it be presented as life or death, but it will be necessary and trepidatious nonetheless. Moving forward by its very definition means to take a step. Here's the good news: God loves to assist those who take the step. What looks camouflaged to you and impossible is crystal clear to God and is possible.

Don't Look Back

> But Jesus said to him, "No one, having put his hand to the plow, and looking back, is fit for the kingdom of God." (Luke 9:62)

There can be no regrets, no doublemindedness, and no going back. When you make the leap, you need to keep walking until you are sprung from your place of "stuck." In 1519 the famous conquistador Captain Hernan Cortés landed in Veracruz to begin his great conquest. Upon arriving he gave the order for his men to "burn the ships." Why did he do that? Would it not have made sense for Cortés to keep a ship or two "just in case" something happened that might require one? What Cortes did was force himself and his men to either succeed or literally die. Retreat was not an option. You see, retreat and doublemindedness are easy when you have that option. We all cling to things that act as our escape hatch or exit strategy. It's our safety net "just in case." If we were honest, we might better say, "This is my safety net just in case I get scared."

I want to encourage you—if you find yourself stuck and vacillating about the way out, consider what I have suggested, and then with God's peace and direction *burn your ships.* Miracles rarely happen when safety nets are securely in place. I understand that some will read this and may do something that could be construed as foolish. Obviously, no one is counseling another to be the fool. However, great steps forward are invariably laced with risk and demand our courage.

Some invariably ask, "What if I interpreted the moment incorrectly and misstep? What if I end up making a poor choice in my attempt to spring loose?" I have come to these conclusions:

God is not trying to penalize us for attempting to move forward in faith. He delights when we demonstrate our willingness to trust Him in new and amazing ways. In other words, I think God really enjoys watching us step in great faith and is moved to help in amazing ways when we do.

God will cause all things to work together for our good (Romans 8:28) when we love Him and are moving according to His purposes. He is the Master at untangling perceived messes.

If you have genuinely disobeyed in your decision-making, then quickly repent before the Lord. Sometimes out of panic, fear, arrogance, and pride, we can certainly make a mess of our lives.

Most of us at one time or another have used a global positioning system (GPS) to find a location. Most of these devices have a voice that can help you drive without taking your eyes off the road. If you happen to make a wrong turn, the voice will often say, "Rerouting to your destination." I have a suspicion that the Holy Spirit's leadership in our life is much like that GPS. It is His preference that we take the most direct route; however, there are times we all have made a wrong turn. The good news is that when we repent and seek His guidance, the Lord has the ability to "reroute" us and get us back on the right track. Don't let the risk deter you from the step. You will be amazed at what the Lord can do.

Chapter Ten

❖ ❖ ❖

The Best Is Yet To Come

On a recent Mother's Day celebration my children wanted to take their mother out for a nice meal at a restaurant she enjoyed. My oldest son is married and has a son, so we checked with my son's wife as well and decided that all the ladies would love eating at a particularly popular Japanese restaurant. One of the boys made the reservation early in the week for 5:00 pm, knowing that it was likely the restaurant would be crowded on a Mother's Day.

I'm not sure how most people approach going to a nice restaurant, but in our house we refrain from eating most of the day in order that we can maximize our dining experience at the favorite restaurant. On this particular day my wife and I simply snacked through the day as we anticipated the great meal we were going to enjoy at 5:00 pm. The family arrived, all eight of us, approximately five minutes before our reservation time. As expected, it was a crowded day at the restaurant. It was obvious that many people had not exercised the foresight our group had by securing their reservations early in the week. We were told it would be a few minutes, which at that moment was understandable because you have to be flexible on a day in which every mom in America may be going out to eat.

After about twenty minutes however, the waiting seemed

inordinately long, so my wife approached the hostess to check on the status. To make a long conversation somewhat shorter, the hostess informed my wife that the wait could be longer, much longer. Another woman was waiting with her group and she interjected at that moment that they had been waiting an hour; their reservation had been made for 4:30 pm. The hostess had told her that there were still people in front of her group. We realized that the restaurant was facilitating walk-ins along with those who had reservations. We did some simple math and realized that the earliest our 5:00 pm reservation would be honored would be at least 6:30 pm and that was not even for sure. My wife kindly asked the hostess, "Well if this is how you are seating people, then why do you take reservations?"

After all, we all thought, a reservation means that there has been an understood expression of agreement on a time and its fulfillment. A reservation means you have confidence that the time you selected *will* be available, not *may* be available. When this was pointed out to the hostess her response was, "That's not how we are defining it today. A reservation today simply means that when you arrive, we will place you in a spot much like 'call-ahead seating.'" In other words, at 4:55 pm when we all arrived, we got a somewhat better placement on a list to be seated, but the promised time of seating was never going to be honored. When faced with waiting this incredibly long time and being quite hungry, the group decided we would try another restaurant nearby and gratefully were able to be seated there almost immediately.

While we were able to salvage Mother's Day to everyone's satisfaction, this experience caused something in me to reflect. I began to realize that appointments and reservations are more important than some might think. In fact, these concepts can actually begin to define a person, a restaurant, or a service. To honor an appointment actually points to one's integrity. You see, no matter how good the food or service this Japanese restaurant may present, because they missed an appointment with me, their integrity in numerous things suddenly got questioned in my mind. If they could not honor a reservation, then how might I know they honor regulations concerning food-handling? If one concept can be redefined on a day, why not another?

I think the concept of punctuality to appointments and reservations touches us all at some point. If we made an appointment with a doctor, realtor, plumber, contractor, pastor, or even the oil-change place, there is a built-in expectation that the time will be honored and respected. Only under unusual circumstances do we normally forgo our desire for timeliness. Punctuality is one point to credibility.

It reminds me of the story of our first United States president, George Washington, who had a reputation of punctuality and timeliness. If he had a meeting with Congress at 12:00 noon, you could count on him walking into the room smartly at 11:59 am. He was known for eating an early dinner, which occurred at 4:00 pm. If you were a guest and invited for dinner, you were expected to be there in your seat on time. It was not uncommon that if guests were late, Washington would start without them. It was reported that on several occasions when guests were late the president would be over half done with the meal and on occasion even finished and moved from the table. President Washington said in reference to this quality, "My cook never asks whether the company has arrived, but whether the hour has come."

> **What God starts in your life He will finish. His integrity is linked to His punctuality and timeliness.**

Paul states something very important about the nature of God, ironically, as he was stuck in a Philippian jail cell.

> Being confident of this very thing, that He who has begun a good work in you will complete it until the day of Jesus Christ; (Philippians 1:6)

What God starts in your life He will finish. His integrity is linked to His punctuality and timeliness. What God starts He will ultimately complete. Consider these Old Testament references to the integrity of God and His timing.

> And the Lord said to Moses, "Has the Lord's arm been shortened? Now you shall see whether what I say will happen to you or not." (Numbers 11:23)

> And the word of the Lord came to me, saying, "Son of man, what is this proverb that you people have about the land of Israel, which says, 'The days are prolonged, and every vision fails'? Tell them therefore, 'Thus says the Lord God: "I will lay this proverb to rest, and they shall no more use it as a proverb in Israel."' But say to them, '"The days are at hand, and the fulfillment of every vision. For no more shall there be any false vision or flattering divination within the house of Israel. For I am the Lord. I speak, and the word which I speak will come to pass; it will no more be postponed; for in your days, O rebellious house, I will say the word and perform it," says the Lord God.'" Again the word of the Lord came to me, saying, "Son of man, look, the house of Israel is saying, 'The vision that he sees is for many days from now, and he prophesies of times far off.' Therefore say to them, 'Thus says the Lord God: "None of My words will be postponed any more, but the word which I speak will be done," says the Lord God.'" (Ezekiel 12:21–28)

> But You, O Lord, shall endure forever, And the remembrance of Your name to all generations. You will arise and have mercy on Zion; For the time to favor her, yes, the set time, has come. (Psalm 102:12–13)

There is a time when God says yes to your promises and your future. His integrity is linked to His punctuality. How do I know this?

Paul again refers to just such a concept in his second letter to the church at Corinth. Again, paradoxically Paul has just finished outlining his many adversities and injustices but then follows up by saying this:

> But as God is faithful, our word to you was not Yes and No. For the Son of God, Jesus Christ, who was preached among you by us—by me, Silvanus, and Timothy—was not Yes and No, but in Him was Yes. For all the promises of God in Him are Yes, and in Him Amen, to the glory of God through us. Now He who establishes us with you in Christ and has anointed us is God, who also has sealed us and given us the Spirit in our hearts as a guarantee. (2 Corinthians 1:18–22)

Whenever a person feels stuck, there are always the subsequent questions of God's integrity, purposes, and will. I can say personally that there are only two aspects of God's nature that I have consistently struggled with. First, I do not struggle with God's omnipotence (all-powerfulness) or His omniscience (all-knowingness) or even His omni-presence (being everywhere at once). I struggle with His speed. If I am stuck and ultimately this is not where I am supposed to be, then why isn't He moving as fast as He could? I addressed some of those possibilities earlier in this book. There may be greater concerns being sanctified in a person's life than simply their comfort levels.

> The believer lives with the confident expectation that the end will always be greater than the beginning because God is in charge of it.

The second area of challenge strikes at the heart of God's integrity. Will He really come through in the end? Will the promises He made come to pass and be manifest in my life as best as I can know them?

For me, the above Scriptures clearly tell me that His will simply cannot be thwarted and what He ultimately has designed for me will indeed come to pass. I like to put it this way: The best is yet to come. No matter where I find myself at the moment, I can confidently say, "I know that something better, greater, more awesome, is just ahead." Don't misunderstand—I am not living with my head in the sand or denying the realities of hardship across the globe, but simply affirming what the Scripture teaches. The believer lives with the confident expectation that the end will always be greater than the beginning because God is in charge of it.

You may be asking, "How can you be so sure? How do you know that the best is yet to come?" I make that statement based on seven principles that I find in the Scriptures that testify to just this point.

The Pattern Of Jesus' Life

The Bible tells us that Jesus is the "firstfruits" of many (1 Corinthians 15:20). His life, while specifically unique because of His divinity, is also a template because of His humanity. No one would argue that Jesus experienced in His short earthly lifetime numerous ups and downs. In fact, the crucifixion account is without dispute, one of the most gruesome yet necessary events that finalized humanity's need for salvation. Yet the story does not end there. Jesus was raised from the dead and ascended into heaven to demonstrate the clear and total victory He held over sin, death, and the grave. As horrifically important as the cross was, the best was just around the corner with the demonstration of the resurrection.

> "O Death, where is your sting? O Hades, where is your victory?" The sting of death is sin, and the strength of sin is the law. But thanks be to God, who gives us the victory through our Lord Jesus Christ. (1 Corinthians 15:55–57)

This is foundationally important to all people who are reading this book. No matter what country you may be living in, no matter what conditions you might find yourself in, no matter the degree of desperation you may be experiencing at this moment, no matter the level of injustice or unfairness that has been unleashed upon you, no matter what the prospects may look like currently to spring you out of your "stuck" circumstance—this first point is immutably true for every Christian believer: *the best is yet to come.*

We tend to forget that. We tend to slip back into the thought that somehow this world is the best God has to offer and that this is all there is. We have conditioned ourselves to expect certain outcomes on this side of eternity and when they do not happen or when they may take longer than we expected or hope, we question God's credibility. This world is not my home. I appreciate the innumerable blessings and experiences I get to enjoy while I am here on this earth, but ultimately this world and its system are not my home. So in the last analysis, I can be sitting, as Paul had been, in a stinky, rat-infested, cave of a prison and still be able to say that all the promises of God are "yes and amen in Him."

The Template Of People's Lives In The Bible

Since the above point has been mentioned, there may be no practical reason to mention others; however, one cannot help but be struck by the many instances of God's people navigating difficult circumstances and experiencing the truth of the best that is yet to come. Noah endures the ridicule of building a boat and experiencing judgment, yet he and his family are saved and repopulate the earth with all its blessings. Abraham moves unexpectedly to a place he has never been, yet the Lord defines it as his inheritance. Joseph is sold into slavery, falsely accused, and left to die in prison, yet God pulls him out to lead in a powerful nation.

Read carefully the exploits of David's "mighty men" and notice what they face and where they ultimately land. David himself starts as a shepherd boy tending a flock enduring a dysfunctional dad, then a demon-oppressed king, and finally a cave with depressing people; yet God brings him to the palace to rule Israel. These are but a few of the stories are recorded in the Scriptures for a reason. God can be trusted, even in earthly circumstances, to bring about a better day than the one you are currently facing.

The Trajectory Of The Gospel

All through history forces have arrayed at different times and places to stamp out the truth of the gospel. The early church perhaps faced some of the most extreme examples of persecution and potential elimination; however, every generation at some place on the planet has experienced the ferocity of evil attempting to obliterate the good news of Jesus Christ. What has been the result? The gospel has not abated nor diminished. In fact, the exact opposite has occurred.

A movement that started with 120 people in an upper room now is approaching two billion adherents. The message of Jesus Christ seems to blossom in the most adverse of situations. The totalitarianism of recent years in China, North Korea, and Russia have done nothing to stop its effect. This is the nature of our God. His work in the earth can come under the most intense afflictions, yet the trajectory is ever forward and victorious. If you are a part of His work, there is no reason to expect any less regardless of your circumstances.

The "Ever-Increasing" Kingdom

Isaiah prophesies of the Messiah's kingdom to be an ever-increasing kingdom (Isaiah 9:7). This can be literally taken as being "unstoppable." The nature of the kingdom of God is unstoppable. It may be paused momentarily. It may look to be detoured or defeated for a moment; but in the final analysis, it cannot be stopped. That kingdom is living and working in you (Luke 17:21). Meditate on that for a moment. This ever-increasing, unstoppable kingdom is resident inside of you as a believer. You cannot be stopped, because this kingdom cannot be stopped.

The Nature of Restoration

When the Bible refers to restoration is not simply underscoring a return of what was lost and a reconstruction of original status, but rather it means that along with original status it actually becomes better than the original (Acts 3:19–21). In other words, God's plan for your life is not simply a recovery of those things stolen or lost, but a reconstruction to a place better than you previously enjoyed. (See Job 42:10.)

While living in Charleston, South Carolina, I came to understand the nature of restoration in a most important way. The city has a great historic district that solicits tourists from all over the world to come and experience. There are neighborhoods with houses that have stood since the 17th and 18th centuries and these houses must be maintained carefully. In order to maintain the historic culture of the city, a special architectural review board was established to maintain, as much as possible, the historic accuracy of these houses. What that means is that before an owner can so much as brush a swipe of paint onto a wall, everything has to be approved. It is the definition of micromanagement. However, the reason the city does this is to maintain accuracy and keep the building as close as possible to its original state. Now there are exceptions that arise in these restoration projects. For example, 17th-century buildings can get modern plumbing, heating, air conditioning, insulated windows, hurricane shutters, hurricane clips, electricity, and—well, you get the point. The building *looks* like the original but in actuality it is *better* than the original. This is how God works in your life. The best is always yet to come.

The Path Of The Righteous

We must take the Scripture seriously and believe what it has promised and stated for the believer. The Bible never promises that every waking moment of our life will be perfect or abundant; however, it does promise that there are certain possibilities that can exist if we choose to walk them out by faith. Paul mentions this very possibility when he writes,

As it is written: "For Your sake we are killed all day long;

129

We are accounted as sheep for the slaughter." Yet in all these things we are *more than conquerors* through Him who loved us. (Romans 8:36–37, emphasis added)

Now thanks be to God who *always* leads us in triumph in Christ, and through us diffuses the fragrance of His knowledge in every place. (2 Corinthians 2:14)

There is an important thread of victory that winds itself all through the Scripture. Even the apostle John would remark,

Whatever is born of God overcomes the world. And this is the victory that has overcome the world—our faith. (1 John 5:4)

God's Nature

I have heard on numerous occasions throughout my years in ministry a thought that goes something like this: "The Lord is trying to get His church back to the book of Acts." It's a compelling thought and one that is seemingly hard to argue. However, I would like to suggest another thought based upon the nature of God, and it is this: "The Lord is trying to get us back not only to the book of Acts—but even greater things." Even Jesus promised His disciples upon leaving that the works He did, they would do, and even greater works (John 14:12).

God's nature is to always eclipse Himself. He delights in doing something greater than He did in previous times. I can only speculate as to why, perhaps it is because there is none who can compete with Him so He must compete with Himself. Whatever He has done in times past, He is more than capable of exceeding that (Ephesians 3:20). This is why the Lord Himself spoke through the prophet and told the people of Israel,

"The glory of this latter temple shall be greater than the former," says the Lord of hosts. "And in this place I will give peace," says the Lord of hosts. (Haggai 2:9)

Perhaps Paul was reflecting upon this very point when he wrote,

But we all, with unveiled face, beholding as in a mirror the glory of the Lord, are being transformed into the same image from glory to glory, just as by the Spirit of the Lord. (2 Corinthians 3:18)

The Lord is always moving His people and His purposes to a better place.

I have a friend whose dad was a pastor that tells the story about a woman, whom upon burial was placed in the casket with a fork in her hand. As the people would walk by to pay their final respects, you could see the puzzled look upon their faces as to why the woman was being buried with a fork in her hand. The answer came when the pastor took to the pulpit and began to eulogize this woman's life. He spoke of her heart to serve, especially in the area of hospitality as she loved to cook and supply meals for guests or visiting speakers. She was a great cook and the meal she prepared would always be the best. Of course, delicious food would always demand seconds, if not thirds, and without exception when time for the dessert came around the people were too full to partake. This hospitable woman would have no part of that and so as she would clear the table for her guests she would always say, "Now everyone, keep your forks—I've saved the best for last." This creative pastor looked down at the casket and then up at the people gathered and said, "This is why the fork was placed in her hands. I wanted everyone to be reminded that the best is yet to come."

Listen, my friend. The best really is yet to come for you too. Whether it is waiting just around the corner only twenty-four hours from now or whether it is in eternity when you meet your Savior face to face, keep your fork. The best is yet to come.

Chapter Eleven

Maintaining A Proper Mentality

Victor Frankl, the notable Viennese psychanalyst, was a prisoner of war in Germany and endured years of humiliation at the hands of the Nazis. He was marched into a Gestapo courtroom and convicted of fabricated crimes against the state. His home was seized. His family was separated. His freedom was denied, and his possessions were confiscated down to his watch and wedding ring. He was shaved, stripped, brought into a courtroom naked, interrogated, and accused falsely. He did nothing to deserve all this. He was made a helpless victim of brutal, evil, and sadistic men. In his book *Man's Search for Meaning* he chronicled the horrors of life for a Jew in a Nazi concentration camp from not only his captors but with each other as well. The book is an analysis of human nature with regard to a person's perspective and actions when placed in the most adverse of circumstances.

History clearly teaches us the evil of the Nazi regime in this time period, but a part of his analysis dealt with how people treated each another when all were under adverse conditions. Some exploited their fellow prisoners as they viewed this horror with a Darwinian "survival of the fittest" mentality, while others processed this circumstance in a totally opposite way as their "better angels" were manifested to help their fellow prisoners. Frankl makes a number of memorable quotes in the book, but one of them resonated with me concerning the mentality of those who find themselves in these "stuck" situations. He writes,

> Everything can be taken from me but one thing, and that is the way I choose to respond to what others do to me. The last of human freedoms is to choose one's attitude in any given set of circumstances, to choose one's own way.

I may not be able to physically change the circumstance I find myself in, but I can choose how I will process it and think about it.

This was never clearer to me than a moment I experienced several years ago at the end of a runway on a commercial flight headed out of Cincinnati. I had boarded a connecting flight to a meeting I was to speak at and had just gotten settled into my seat when I glanced at my wristwatch to check the time. Back in those days a wristwatch had the clock face that displayed the normal 1 through 12 circular pattern, as well as a small rectangle off to the side that showed the abbreviated weekday and date. That day was Tuesday the seventh, so the rectangle should have displayed TUE 7. On this occasion I was startled to see something in that rectangle that was completely shocking. It read DIE 7. I shook my head and looked again. It said, DIE 7. My heart started to race. Was this some miraculous sign from God that this plane was about to go down today and this was my warning sign to stop the plane? Was I to stand up and look like the village idiot signaling a problem to the flight attendants about an emergency that had yet to take place? Were they going to believe the watch as I pointed to its face in sheer terror? Panic was starting to grip me. I really wasn't sure what to do.

❖ ❖ ❖

> I may not be able to physically change the circumstance I find myself in, but I can choose how I will process it and think about it.

The plane was just seconds from the pilot racing the rpms to the engines that would hurl us down the runway. I decided to quickly pull the stem of the watch to see if there were any other divine signs located inside the rectangle upon twisting the stem. To my amazement, the three-letter abbreviation which followed DIE was TUE, after which was MIT and then WED. What I had not realized was the English abbreviations for the day of the week followed the German abbreviations. *Dienstag* was the German word for Tuesday and *Mittwoch* the word for Wednesday. I did not know I owned a German watch until those abbreviations appeared on the face of the watch. Gratefully, as it turned out, I did not die that day and landed safely at my destination. What I did learn in that panicked moment of terror was how easily a simple misreading of a circumstance can cause not only emotional upheaval but also a potentially disastrous decision. I found out that my mental discipline with regard to my future may not have been as settled as I may have thought.

> **What you focus on is what you will think about and what you think about is what you will ultimately become or where you will ultimately go.**

Why do I mention this point in a book whose premise is that people are stuck and desire to move forward? I mention it because your mentality will place a large and significant role as to how you handle your "stuck" moment and how you navigate out.

As he thinks in his heart, so is he. (Proverbs 23:7)

There is a simple biblical syllogism that is important to understand. What you focus on is what you will think about and what you think about is what you will ultimately become or where you will ultimately go. It's unfortunate that many people will either never get freed from their present circumstances or will be unable to maintain their current walk of freedom because they have not maintained a proper mentality. People tend to view life only in the context of their crisis, their obstacle, their problem, or their pitfall. If that mentality is never seized and broken, the person begins to live, think, and function for the next crisis rather than their emerging purpose and promise.

There may be no better illustration than the children of Israel themselves as they were positioned to head into the Promised Land on the first attempt in Numbers 13 and 14. The nation was on the brink of a great destiny after experiencing centuries stuck in the slavery of Egypt. They had seen amazing signs and wonders wrought by God to bring them out with a mighty miracle of deliverance. Yet despite having these amazing moments of testimony, their mentality had not changed.

The story begins with the Lord commanding Moses to send men into the land to "spy" out the situation (Numbers 13:2). The account never records the Lord stating the reasons as to why this needed to be done, but I surmise that the Lord wanted the people to get a vision of the future that was ahead of them. Later in the chapter Moses commands these spies to go into the land and more or less give an evaluation of what they were facing (13:17–20). That seems reasonable at face value, but honestly it was beyond the scope of what the Lord had commanded. His command was simply "Get a vision of the promise." Moses added, "I want to know the details and especially the problems." I respect Moses as a leader and the amazing ways God used him in delivering the people of Israel, but candidly, his addition capitulated to a mentality that had yet to be renewed. Perhaps Moses had been affected by the rebellion of chapter 12. Perhaps he was pragmatically developing a strategy of entrance rather than the simplicity of obeying. Whatever the motive, the spies came back with some good news and some bad news (Numbers 13:27–29). This type of report concerning the land caused a mentality to ripple through the ranks and infect the entire nation.

But the men who had gone up with him said, "We are not able to go up against the people, for they are stronger than we." And they gave the children of Israel a bad report of the land which they had spied out, saying, "The land through which we have gone as spies is a land that devours its inhabitants, and all the people whom we saw in it are men of great stature. There we saw the giants (the descendants of Anak came from the giants); and we were like grasshoppers in our own sight, and so we were in their sight." (Numbers 13:31–33)

However you choose to think, is what you will eventually become and where you will eventually go. This is why it is vital that you maintain a proper mentality when you are stuck.

Your ability to move forward is far more internal than external in most cases. Thomas à Kempis said, "Live in such a way that there is always something deeper on the inside than anyone could ever see on the outside." The question, of course is "How does one do that?" How do you maintain a proper mentality when you are frustrated, aggravated, panicked, and fearful sitting in your "stuck" place?

Remember: You Are Not The First To Face Such Moments

When Elijah was chased by Jezebel and sitting under a tree pondering his circumstances, he fell into the "I'm the only one" syndrome. He thought that he was the only one left who might be righteous as well as the only one facing such a challenging moment. The Lord rebuked him for such thoughts. We all have those tendencies to believe that "I am the only one" who has ever faced such a moment. If crises in people's lives could be voted upon, we often feel as if ours must be the worst. The truth is that yours is probably not the worst and you are not the first to face difficulty and prevail.

George Bernard Shaw, while not a Christian in any orthodox sense, summed up this tendency in his usual acerbic manner when he wrote,

This is the true joy of life, being used for a purpose recognized by yourself as a mighty one, being a force of nature instead of a feverish, selfish little clod of ailments and grievances complaining that the world will not devote itself to making you happy.

Shaw was brutal in his analysis but nonetheless accurate. We all face difficulties and must exert mental toughness when those moments arrive.

Keep A Positive, Faith-Filled Confession

People have often asked me how to change or maintain a way of thinking. Our natural inclination is to believe that to change a thought, one must try to think different thoughts. That is almost impossible to do. Changing and maintaining thoughts occur when a person verbalizes (speaks) what God has promised and not simply what he is seeing. I am not suggesting that you deny the reality of what you are facing, but rather affirm the reality of what God has said yes to. You must begin to filter *fear* out of your vocabulary.

For some people the single greatest obstacle to their release is their mouth. Is it not interesting that the generation of Israelites who articulated their fears concerning the giants in the land had to be removed in order for a generation to arise who were able to say, "We are well able to move into the land"?

Optimism in our confession really costs us little and is an incredible tool in maintaining a proper mentality. A poster in the locker room of the Phoenix Suns reads, "The game is scheduled, we have to play it, so we might as well win." Perhaps we all need a sign in our bedrooms that stares us in the face as we awaken to a new day that says, "Your life is where it is, you have to live it, you might as well believe it's going to be fantastic." No one can force you to be optimistic. You alone have the ability to decide how you will approach your life and circumstances.

There Is More At Work Than Just You

Sometimes our challenges are birthing places for great testimonies that can be used to speak to others and potentially help them. A crisis gives you the opportunity to demonstrate to a watching world just how committed you are to the plan of God no matter what is thrown at you or where you find yourself. Christianity works great for everyone on a mountaintop, but what about when you are stuck in a valley? When you are aware that God is at work in some greater way beyond your personal moment, it can help maintain your focus and thinking.

Mental Tenacity Takes Exercise

Just as your muscles are developed through strength producing exercises, so your tenacity and perseverance are developed through situations that demand a mental toughness. Your "stuck" moment is actually a question. How badly do you really want the will of God? Jesus was afforded numerous shortcuts to the Father's plan but rejected them all to accomplish God's purpose in His life. You are facing a "stuck" moment that may be an exercise in greater challenges to move you to a destiny. Determine to remain tenacious and use the moment as a mental exercise in developing those mental muscles.

Some years ago I did a word study on the Hebrew word for *meditate*. Meditation is biblical when you mentally dwell on the Word of God. If you follow the etymology of the word, it actually gives the sense of "imagination." In other words, what will you allow your mind to see? The truth is, whatever your mind begins to see, you will begin to say. Philippians 4:8 tells us—whatever things are true, noble, just, pure, lovely, and of good report, meditate on these things.

I played baseball in high school and some in college. A key to being an effective hitter is visualizing the bat connecting with the ball. The problem enters the picture when the pitcher you're facing can throw the ball over ninety miles per hour. You want to say, "I can't hit a ball traveling that fast." However, that is the greatest mistake. You must see yourself connecting with that baseball and begin to say, "I can hit this in the gap for extra bases." In much the same way, you must see yourself as God sees you and calls you, which is *victorious, conquering*, and overcoming. That scene in your mind that was received from God's Word will begin to change your confession and then your thoughts.

I was listening to a psychologist recently who coined the term *awfulization*. He defined it as taking a thought and letting it run to its most awful conclusion and then acting upon it. Many people practice *awfulization*. They become convinced that it will become reality before it even happens. These are the thoughts that must be seized and cast down. That happens only through mental tenacity.

This Too Shall Pass

All our afflictions are temporary. Tell yourself that the moment you are in is not forever. Temporal things are just that—temporary. Your circumstances are always subject to change; however, God's Word is forever established in the heavens for all eternity. What He has said can be counted on. Keep that front and center. Resist overly praying about the problem. Yes, the problem is real and God doesn't mind your lifting the need up to Him, but is your prayer only about the problem? God is not moved by your moaning but rather your faith. Quit giving your problems and circumstances more time before God than your faith and your future. Practice gratitude in the midst of challenges.

Keeping your thoughts on target will be a challenge. It is for everyone. But those who commit to maintaining a proper mentality will almost without fail find themselves moving forward in life.

My wife recently completed a job as a residential property manager of an upscale condo community. These condos were located on the harbor in Charleston, South Carolina, and it had, literally, a million-dollar view. The people who lived at these condos were people of great financial means. These condos were mostly second homes for the residents of the property. Wealthy people are interesting to hang around. The vast majority of the time wealthy people are very self-sufficient, autonomous, independent, demanding, sophisticated, and shrewd. There are, of course, pleasant exceptions, but wealth definitely causes a person to think differently. On occasion I would attend special events at the condos with my wife and have opportunity to visit with many of them on a social basis. I would ask all sorts of questions because I found most people love to talk about themselves, so I simply opened the door to learning what made a self-made millionaire tick. After listening to their stories of fame, celebrity, and acquisition of wealth, my wife and I would often remark at how wealthy people simply "think" differently.

The one exception, however, was when a hurricane was headed our direction. Tracie and I had experienced several of these moments in the past twenty-three years of living on the coast, so our mentality was strategic and patient as we listened to the reports updated every five to six hours. These millionaires, normally a disciplined group of thinkers, were suddenly in a panic as many, having moved down south from the north, had never navigated such a moment. It was fascinating to say the least. All their monetary knowledge and wealth wisdom suddenly did them no good in the prospect of a storm. They panicked and allowed fear to set in at that moment. Their lack of mental discipline was exploited during the storm.

In much the same way, your storm will challenge your thinking. But storms pass. Keep that front and center and you will weather those paralyzing moments victoriously.

Conclusion

I started this book with a personal crisis story that took place while I was seated in a pizza restaurant feeling stuck beyond possible deliverance. As with any personal story, the details themselves would consume far more pages than most people would care to read. However, to synopsize the opening cliffhanger of the introduction I can say several things that are important in conclusion.

As I mentioned, not every "stuck" moment concludes in a way you might initially want or even map out. Sometimes God is working paradoxically and providentially beyond your current understanding or comprehension. In other words, His ending may not always look like the ending you are writing in your mind. The land we had miraculously purchased was never used to build a church. Because of the reduction of people during that season and the unfolding and blossoming of another aspect of my calling at the same time, it became apparent that a new facility simply wasn't going to happen.

Sometimes God is working paradoxically and providentially beyond your current understanding or comprehension.

Yes, there were many questions on top of the ones that swirled at the beginning of this whole event. Why was that land secured and in such

miraculous ways and then seemingly "stuck"?

The answer actually came a number of years later when through another set of miraculous events the land was eventually sold (interestingly, to a man who had a vision to build a non-denominational revival center on it. Doesn't the Lord have an ironic sense of humor?). The equity, through the monies of the sale and by the decision of the board of directors in my church, were used to launch the next season of ministry into which my wife and I were called. In fact, had it not been for that gracious and generous act of that board, I'm not sure I would be sitting at this laptop now typing out these words and traveling across this nation and the globe encouraging, equipping, and empowering Christian leaders for their vision and calling. I moved forward, but my movement forward was in God's plan and not my own.

> ❖ ❖ ❖
>
> **The irreducible point to moving forward is simply this: do you desire God's plan, His purposes, and His will?**

Perhaps this is the best place to conclude the premise of this book. The irreducible point to moving forward is simply this: do you desire God's plan, His purposes, and His will? If you do, then rest assured that this passion will be the environment God will work in to lead you out of your "stuck" place. How passionately, or perhaps better said commonly, how *badly* do you want His will? When people run for high political office, especially the presidency, it is often asked of them, "Do you have a 'fire in the belly'?" People want to know if there is an uncommon desire in the candidate to apprehend this office and work this job, or will this only be like a hobby? It's an important question, because in the days we are living in, any elected office runs the high likelihood of being smeared and harassed as a public official. If you don't have a fire in the belly, you probably won't survive. The same could be said of getting "unstuck." Do you have a fire in the belly for God's plan, His will, and His purposes? The Lord has incredible possibilities for His people, but are you sold out to what He wants and not necessarily what you have designed? Because if you are, then a way forward will be revealed.

I remember a story a seasoned preacher told years ago concerning a zoological expedition to South America in search of new reptiles for display. The reptiles represented a large swath of species that included the highly poisonous bushmaster snake, whose venom is toxic within seconds. The scientists put the snake into a box and stored it appropriately in the ship to sail back to the states. In the middle of the voyage, upon inspection, the scientists found that the deadly snake had escaped. Immediately a search was instituted across the ship to locate the snake, but it couldn't be found. Finally a party of searchers reached the very bottom of the ship and found the snake. It was curled up around a metal anchor dead. But how?

The snake had few natural predators and certainly no one on board was willing to face it in a dark space alone. Suddenly they heard out of the darkness a "meow." There only a few feet away was a momma cat sitting next to her two babies, stuck in a corner. The point of the story is this: If there is a big enough reason why, you'll do whatever it takes to prevail.

Victor Frankl put it this way: "He who has a 'why' to live can endure any 'how.'" You can move forward if your passion is to follow the purposes of God. Paul said it like this:

> I consider that the sufferings of this present time are not worthy to be compared with the glory which shall be revealed in us. (Romans 8:18)

I have personally come to the conclusion that Paul was referencing not only eternity but also the work of the Lord temporally as we press forward in His plans. There is a glory of His presence and affirmation that will be made manifest for all to see as we pursue His will even when it seems as if circumstances are stuck, impossible, and certainly not what we had envisioned.

I can remember with almost crystal-clear clarity a 1984 Olympic women's marathon race that took place in Los Angeles. Women's marathons are not normally the highest-viewed events watched by the public, but this one captured everyone's attention. In fact, in a twisted way it became the one you wanted to look away from, the one that made you groan to look at but just had to watch. The runner's name was Gabriela Anderson, a Swiss runner who would eventually finish 37th, but her finish was far more memorable than that of the actual winner.

For several gut-wrenching minutes, viewers started to wonder not whether she would finish the race but whether she would survive it. As Anderson came out of the tunnel to the finish line with only a few hundred yards left in the race, she began to stumble and sway, almost giving the appearance of being drunk, but her athleticism would dismiss those thoughts swiftly. The Olympic assistants saw what was happening and were obviously uncertain as to what to do. If they touched her she would be disqualified, but if they allowed her to continue, whatever was wrong might kill her.

Gabriela's final lap around the stadium seemed to take forever. It was as if time stood still as the world watched what was happening. She had trained for not only a strong finish but also as a top contender. Those aspirations had now vanished, and the question was simply "Can she finish?" One Olympic doctor would comment later, "If it had been one of my athletes, I wouldn't have let this happen. There were tears in my eyes. I was saying, 'O God, what a mess this is!' It was the dilemma of all time. Do you intervene and pull her out of the race fearing for her life, or do you let her go and see how it ends and potentially have blood on your hands? She had just run twenty-six miles—why not let her run another four hundred meters?" As Gabriela approached the finish line her pace quickened and her arms began swinging wildly. As she crossed the finish line she collapsed and fell into the arms of Olympic officials.

Gratefully, it was later diagnosed that Gabriela had suffered mild dehydration rather than a debilitating heatstroke. But in the end Gabriela redefined courage and demonstrated a triumph of desire. She wanted to finish this race, and finish it she did. She wasn't the winner who would stand on the podium with a gold medal, but she was the winner in the eyes of everyone who watched the race that day across the globe. In fact, no one remembers the winner, but everyone remembers Gabriela.

Stories like these are the context of what it means to move forward. You plan, you strive, you scramble to find ways to shake loose and press forward, but ultimately your fulfillment and contentment come in knowing that God is at work bringing His good plan to pass in your life. It is my contention that this character trait has been lost and is sorely needed in the era we are currently in. No, not every situation shakes out the way you think it will or even should, but that is not the

❖ ❖ ❖

You are moving forward not for your agenda but rather God's.

point. You are moving forward not for your agenda but rather God's. And as I mentioned previously, even if your situation is found to be one of the most desperate imaginable, for the believer you will always move forward in Him.

A declaration I ran across some years ago has ministered to me on numerous occasions. The background as to its source is shaky. Some say the author of this work is a Rwandan man who perhaps a century ago was forced by his tribe to either renounce Christ or face certain death. You might say he was facing the ultimate "stuck" moment of his life. He refused to renounce Christ. He was committed to the Lord's will. He was killed on the spot. The night before this tragic event he had written the personal commitment declaration "The Fellowship of the Unashamed," which was found in his room. Author Bob Moorhead would eventually write this declaration in his 1995 book *Words Aptly Spoken*. It has become familiar to many and may be the best conclusion to this book.

I am part of the fellowship of the unashamed. I have Holy Spirit power. The die has been cast. I have stepped over the line. The decision has been made. I am a disciple of His. I won't look back, let up, slow down, back away, or be still.

My past is redeemed. My present makes sense. My future is secure. I'm finished with low living, sight walking, small planning, smooth knees, colorless dreams, tamed visions, worldly talking, cheap giving, and dwarfed goals.

I no longer need preeminence, prosperity, position, promotions, applause, or popularity. I don't have to be right, first, tops, recognized, praised, regarded, or rewarded. I now live by faith, lean on His presence, walk by patience, am uplifted by prayer, and labor by power.

My pace is set. My gait is fast. My goal is heaven. My road is narrow. My way rough. My companions few. My guide is reliable, and my mission is clear.

I cannot be bought, compromised, detoured, lured away, turned back, deluded, or delayed. I will not flinch in the face of sacrifice, hesitate in the presence of the adversary, negotiate at the table of the enemy, pander at the pool of popularity, or meander in the maze of mediocrity.

I won't give up, shut up, let up, until I've stayed up, stored up, prayed up, paid up, preached up for the cause of Christ.

I am a disciple of Jesus. I must go till He comes, give 'til I drop, preach till all know, and work till He stops me. And when He comes for His own, He'll have no problem recognizing me. My banner will be clear.

This is the hymn of those who will forever move forward. There is a reason we define a Christian's homegoing as "graduation day." It's because although each one of us is stuck in this mortal body, there will come a day when we are liberated in the eternal sense and forever "unstuck" by the shackles of this world. His children always move forward.

May it be said of us all these very words.

About The Author

D r. Kevin Baird is the Executive Director of Legacy Christian Ministries in Jacksonville, Florida. After a dramatic conversion at age eighteen and subsequent call to ministry a few months later, he was holding revival meetings, speaking on college campuses, and eventually became a lead pastor at age twenty-four. Dr. Baird has been well-educated, earning his B.A. in Religion & Philosophy; a M.Div. in Historical Theology; and a D.Min. in History of Christian Thought, focusing his project dissertation on John Wesley's leadership of the Methodist Renewal Movement in the 18th Century. His ministry experience has been extensive through more than forty years as a lead pastor, church planter, national conference speaker, college professor, talk radio host, biblical worldview advocate in public policy, popular blog writer (www.drkevinbaird.com), and media analyst on culture. He has been an invited contributor to *Fox and Friends*, as well as other national media outlets, including radio, newspapers, and cable news networks. He is the co-host of the new podcast, **THE BAIRD & BAIRD PODCAST,** with his son, Pastor Clayton Baird, discussing life and ministry from a bi-generational angle. Currently, along with his traveling schedule, Dr. Baird is an active professor at Christian Life School of Theology (Pensacola, Florida), as well as Southeastern University (Jacksonville, Florida campus). He is also the Director of

Pastoral Ministries for the Florida Family Policy Council, which serves the 12,600 evangelical churches in Florida.

Dr. Baird and his wife Tracie, are currently traveling across the globe seeking to encourage, empower, and equip Christian believers and leaders in personal and professional growth. Tracie Baird is an accomplished teacher and speaker focusing on her newly created curriculum, ***The Roadmap to Freedom: Persevering from Your Past to Your Purpose***. She has ministered to countless people across the globe in local church settings, conferences, and seminars. Her humor, honesty, and authenticity has set people free to pursue their purpose in God with fresh vision. Her transparency, coupled with her sound biblical training, provides a powerful atmosphere of healing and wholeness. Together, the Baird's form a unique ministry team, impacting multitudes of people for the Kingdom of God in a profound way.

The Baird's have been married for over forty years and have two sons, one daughter, two "daughters-in-love," and three amazing grandsons.

If you would like more information, or to schedule the Baird's (Kevin or Tracie) for speaking at your local church, conference, or event, you may contact them at:
bairdk370@gmail.com.

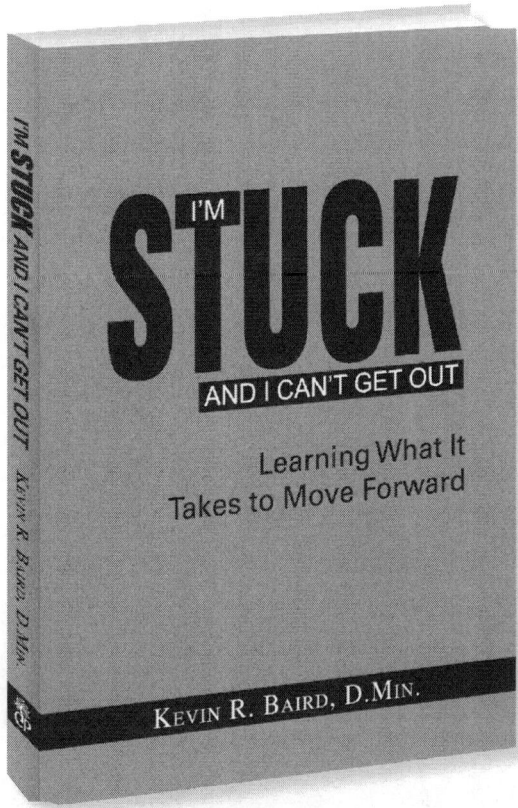

I'M STUCK
AND I CAN'T GET OUT

Learning What It
Takes to Move Forward

KEVIN R. BAIRD, D.MIN.

To order more copies of

I'M
STUCK
AND I CAN'T GET OUT

contact CertaPublishing.com

❐ Order online at CertaBooks.com/Bookstore

❐ Email: bairdk370@gmail.com

Also available on Amazon.com

Certa
PUBLISHING